KINGDOM BIBLE STUDY

PROGRAM FOR SUNDAY SCHOOLS

Laying the Right Foundation for a Future Generation

9-10 Years

Abraham John

Genesis Project 126

BIBLE STUDY PROGRAM FOR SUNDAY SCHOOL CHILDREN (AGES 9-10 YEARS OLD)

Copyright © 2025 Abraham John

Published by Tree of Life
For The Kingdom University

www.TheKingdomUniversity.org
email: admin@TheKingdomUniversity.org
1(800) 558 5020

ISBN: 978-1-948330-52-7

Printed in the United States of America

All emphasis or additions within Scripture quotations are the author's own.

Unless otherwise indicated, all Scripture quotations are taken from the New King James Version of the Holy Bible. Copyright ©1995-2010, The Zondervan Corporation. All Rights Reserved.

Scripture quotations marked CEV are taken from the Contemporary English Version (Bible for Today's Family). Copyright ©American Bible Society 1991, 1992, 1995; Anglicizations British and Foreign Bible; Society 1996. All rights reserved.

Scripture quotations marked ESV® are from The Holy Bible, English Standard Version® (ESV®) ©2001 by Crossway, a publishing ministry of Good News Publishers. All rights reserved.

Scripture quotations are taken from the Amplified Bible® (AMPC®) © 1954, 1958, 1962, 1964, 1965, 1987 by The Lockman Foundation. Used by permission lockman.org

All rights reserved. No part of this book may be reproduced or transmitted in any form or by any means, electronic or mechanical—including photocopying, recording, or by any information storage and retrieval system without permission in writing from the author.

Please direct your inquiries to admin@TheKingdomUniversity.org

TABLE OF CONTENTS

Introduction to the Bible Study Program — 9

BOOK 1: CHILDREN 9-10 YEARS OLD — 11

PART 1: WHO AM I? — 13

Lesson 1: I Am A Spirit Living In A Body — 15
Lesson 2: I Am A Child Of God — 18
Lesson 3: I Will Live Forever — 21
Lesson 4: I Am A Boy Made In God's Image — 23
Lesson 5: I Am A Girl And I Am Someone Special — 26
Lesson 6: I Am Just Like My Heavenly Father — 29
Lesson 7: I Function Like My Heavenly Father — 32
Lesson 8: I Can Imagine — 35
Lesson 9: I Am A King — 38
Lesson 10: I Am A Queen — 41
Lesson 11: I Am Creative Like My Father — 44
Lesson 12: I Am Being Trained: To Become A Man, A Husband, And A Father — 47
Lesson 13: I Am Being Trained: To Become A Woman, A Wife, And A Mother — 51
Lesson 14: I Am Created To Bring Life And Be Productive — 54
Lesson 15: I Am Created To Conceive And Give Birth To God's Purpose On The Earth — 58
Lesson 16: I Am Beautiful In My Spirit, My Soul, And My Body — 61
Lesson 17: I Am An Original — 65
Lesson 18: I Speak Like My Heavenly Father — 68
Lesson 19: I Am Loved By My Heavenly Father — 72

TABLE OF CONTENTS

PART 2: WHY AM I HERE? 75

Lesson 20: I Am Created In God's Image And Likeness 77
Lesson 21: I Am Created To Have Dominion 80
Lesson 22: My Purpose Is Connected To The Earth 83
Lesson 23: I Am A Manager And Influencer 86
Lesson 24: I Am A Builder And Repairer 89
Lesson 25: I Am Called To Lead 92
Lesson 26: I Can Subdue And Overcome 95
Lesson 27: I Am Called To Excel And Grow 98
Lesson 28: I Can Be Productive And Fruitful 101
Lesson 29: I Am Here To Build And Bring Back 104
Lesson 30: I Have Gifts And Talents 107
Lesson 31: I Am A Problem Solver 110
Lesson 32: I Am Fearless 113
Lesson 33: I Am Part Of A Bigger Picture 116
Lesson 34: I Make A Difference 119
Lesson 35: I Need Wisdom And Help 122
Lesson 36: I Am A Blessing 125
Lesson 37: I Protect And Care For 128
Lesson 38: I Rebuild Relationships 131
Lesson 39: I Am Created To Rule In My Area 134
Lesson 40: I Represent God's Kingdom 137
Lesson 41: Creation Is Waiting For Me 140

TABLE OF CONTENTS

PART 3: WHERE DID I COME FROM?   143

Lesson 42: I Come From God   145

Lesson 43: I Come From Heaven   148

Lesson 44: I Come From The Kingdom Of Heaven   151

Lesson 45: I Am A Kingdom Ambassador   154

Lesson 46: I Am Made/Created By God Almighty   157

Lesson 47: I Am Skilfully And Wonderfully Made   160

Lesson 48: I Need Th e Kingdom Of God   163

Lesson 49: God Sent Me To Do His Work   166

Lesson 50: Nobody Else Can Do What I Do   169

Lesson 51: God Needs Me Here On Earth   172

Lesson 52: The Earth Is My Permanent Home   175

MORE BOOKS AND RESOURCES   179

INTRODUCTION TO THE BIBLE STUDY PROGRAM

Train up a child in the way he should go, and when he is old he will not depart from it (Proverbs 22:6).

The Tree of Life children's Bible Study Program is thoughtfully designed to lay a firm spiritual foundation in the hearts and minds of young children during their most formative years.

Rooted in the principles of Kingdom Education, this program aims to help children discover their identity, understand their purpose, and know their origin.

At the core of the program are three foundational books authored by Dr. Abraham John. These include the following:

1. Who Am I?
2. Why Am I Here?
3. Where Did I Come From?

Knowing that every human being will ask these questions and the importance of it, God Almighty answered all of them in the very first chapter of the Bible. As I share in my books and teachings, Genesis 1:26 is the **purpose statement** for mankind, given by our Creator. We've neglected it, thinking it's just an Old Testament creation story.

Your spirit came into this world fully aware and with the knowledge of who you are and why you were sent to this earth. Instead of welcoming and nurturing that spirit to release what they were sent here for, most children are trained in the ways of this world. The environment in which we were born and raised plays a role in brainwashing and forming a wrong mindset in us.

INTRODUCTION TO THE BIBLE STUDY PROGRAM

To be born a male or a female is a natural process, but becoming a man or woman is intentional, just like no one becomes a pilot, a doctor, or a scientist by birth. They have to go through intense training to become that.

The lessons are directed to both boys and girls independently of the topic, because both genders need to understand the respective role of each other in order to live in harmony with one another and fulfill their God given purpose.

The curriculum is designed as a repeating annual cycle, allowing students to revisit these vital themes each year. This repetition deepens their understanding as they grow and mature, preparing them to carry a clear sense of identity, purpose, and divine origin, as they transition through each stage of their development.

Four Key Kingdom Educational Stages

This complete program is aligned with four key educational stages in the Kingdom framework, being the following:

- **Kindergarten Stage (Ages 0 to 5 years old)**: These early years focus on laying a strong foundation for their identity, purpose, and origin. Through engaging visuals, brief thematic introductions, and songs, young children begin to explore fundamental questions such as Who am I?, Why am I here?, and Where did I come from?. They are divided into two groups in order to address their respective developmental needs:

  » Infants and Toddlers (0 to 2 years old), and
  » Preschoolers (3 to 5 years old).

INTRODUCTION TO THE BIBLE STUDY PROGRAM

- **Primary Level (Ages 6 to 12 years old)**

  » Lower Primary (6 to 8 years old) : At this stage, children build upon the foundation laid in preschool, deepening their understanding of identity, calling, and life purpose. This is achieved through the use of the original three-book set, along with accompanying coloring books that reinforce key themes in an engaging and age-appropriate way.

  » Upper Primary (9 to 12 years old) : At this stage, children strengthen the foundation laid in earlier years and begin to explore their unique gifts, strengths, and calling. They are encouraged to identify their personal strengths and understand how these relate to their life's purpose, helping them form a clearer sense of direction and identity.

- **Secondary Level (Ages 13 to 17)**: This phase focuses on training and development, equipping senior school scholars to nurture their talents and prepare for a life of excellence ahead. The goal is to help them hone their gifts in anticipation of fulfilling their respective callings. These youthful scholars are divided into two age groups:

  » Lower Secondary (12 to 14 years old) and
  » Upper Secondary (15 to 17 years old).

- **College and University Level (Ages 18-plus)**: With a solid foundation in their identity and purpose, students at the university level are empowered to apply their learning in real-world contexts. Through mentoring and coaching, they are supported as they exercise dominion in their specific areas of calling; ultimately becoming leaders and agents of transformation in their respective fields of further study and endeavor.

The Tree of Life children's Bible Study Program is a spiritual journey designed to raise confident, purpose-driven young adults who know who they are, why they're here, and where they come from; and who are later sent out to fulfill their Divine purpose and callings in life.

Abraham John
Tree of Life

BOOK 1

Children 9-10 Years old

PART ONE
Who am I?

LESSON 1: I AM A SPIRIT LIVING IN A BODY

Learning Objectives:

By the end of this lesson, children will be able to:

1. Identify that they are spirit, soul, and body, recognizing that their spirit is what makes them truly alive.
2. Explain that God created human beings with a body formed from the earth and given life by His Spirit.
3. Recognize that true life comes from God's Spirit.
4. Understand and express that their body is a special home for God's Spirit.

Story: The Clay Boy

Prince was a curious little boy who loved learning new things. One day, he watched a movie about how the world was made. He was amazed to see that God made the first person from dust! Prince ran to his mom. "Mom! Did God really make a person from dirt?" he asked.

"Yes," Mom smiled. "Our bodies come from the earth because our Purpose is connected to Earth." She opened the Bible and read: **"Then the Lord God formed man from the dust of the ground, and breathed into his nostrils the breath of life; and man became a living being."** *Genesis 2:7*

"Wow! That's so cool!" said Prince, and he ran to get some clay. He rolled the clay and made a little person with arms, legs, a head, and feet. Then he blew on it… but it didn't move. Prince looked confused. "Why didn't it come to life?"

Mom sat beside him and said, "Only God can give life. It's not just the body that matters—it's the spirit inside that makes us alive, and your body is the temple of the Holy Spirit Who is in you."

Prince's eyes grew big. "So my body is like a house, and God's Spirit lives inside me?" "That's right," Mom said. "God made your body, but He also gave you a spirit. That's what makes you really alive."

Prince looked at his clay boy and whispered, "You're not alive… but I am—and God lives in me!"

Questions:

1. How did God make the first person?
2. What happened when Prince blew on his clay person?
3. Who gives life to us?
4. What lives inside your body that makes you alive?

Memory Verse

"It is the Spirit who gives life; the flesh profits nothing." John 6:63 (NKJV)

Activity: "Make Your Clay Person"

What you need: Clay or play dough and your hands to shape it!

What to do:

1. Make a small person out of clay or play dough.
2. Give it arms, legs, a head, and a body.
3. Talk about how your clay person can't move or live by itself.
4. Remember how God gives you a special spirit that makes you alive!

Notes:

_____

_____

_____

_____

_____

LESSON 2: I AM A CHILD OF GOD

Learning Objectives:

By the end of this lesson, children will be able to:

1. See that they are children of God, knowing that everyone who receives Jesus becomes part of God's family.
2. Explain that God's love is unconditional and forever, even when we make mistakes.
3. Know the difference between worldly love and godly love, comparing human examples with God's loving character.
4. Find God as a loving Father (Abba) Who adopts and cares for His children.
5. Show belonging through reflecting their identity as God's beloved child.

Story: God's Family

John loved watching shows about animals. He liked seeing how animals take care of their families. One day, John saw a show about lions. At first, it was fun! The lions played and ran around. But then something sad happened. A little lion cub tried to eat before the daddy lion, and the father growled and chased him away. The little lion cub had to find food by itself.

Although John understood that this behavior is normal in the Lion's Kingdom, still he felt sad and sorry for the little lion cub. "What if God treated His children like that?" he thought.

That night, while reading his Bible, a passage popped up before his eyes, and he read, **"But God demonstrates His own love toward us, in that while we were still sinners, Christ died for us."** *Romans 5:8(NKJV)*

"Wait!" he said. "God's love isn't like the lions!" In God's Kingdom, things are different. Jesus, the King, Who gave up His life so we could be part of God's family. John looked up at the stars and whispered, "Thank You, Father. Thank You for always loving me."

Questions:

1. How did the daddy lion treat the little lion cub?
2. How is God's love different from the lion's love?
3. What does it mean to be a child of God?
4. Why did Jesus die for us?

Memory Verse

"But as many as received Him, to them He gave the right to become children of God." John 1:12(NKJV)

Activity: "Family Love Drawing"

What you need: Paper and crayons or colored markers

What to do:

1. Draw a picture of your family showing love—like hugging, playing, or helping each other.
2. Talk about how God loves His family (us) very much, even more than we can imagine!
3. Remember, you are part of God's big family!

Notes:

LESSON 3: I WILL LIVE FOREVER

Learning Objectives:

By the end of this lesson, children will be able to:

1. Explain that Jesus died and rose again, understanding that His resurrection gives us the promise of eternal life.
2. Express hope and joy in knowing they will live forever with Jesus.
3. Know that eternal life is a gift from God for those who believe in Jesus.
4. Describe heaven as a place with no sadness, pain, or death, based on biblical promises.

Story: Osvaldo's Joyful Night

One quiet evening, Osvaldo sat next to his mom as she read the Bible. She told him the story of how Jesus died on the cross. Osvaldo's eyes filled with tears. His mom gave him a big hug. "It's okay to feel sad," she said kindly. "Jesus did that because He loves us more than anything. But guess what?" she smiled, "That's not how the story ends!" She opened the Bible and read: **"Jesus said to her, 'I am the resurrection and the life. He who believes in Me, though he may die, he shall live. And whoever lives and believes in Me shall never die.'"** *John 11:25-26(NKJV)*

Osvaldo's eyes got wide. "So... Jesus came back to life?" "That's right!" said his mom. "Jesus is alive! And because He lives, we don't have to be afraid of dying. One day, we'll live forever with Him."

Osvaldo felt hope fill his heart. "What will it be like to live with God forever?" he asked. His mom turned to the last part of the Bible and read: **"And God will wipe away every tear from their eyes; there shall be no more death, nor sorrow, nor crying. There shall be no more pain..."** Revelation 21:4(NKJV)

"Wow!" whispered Osvaldo. "That sounds like the happiest place ever." That night, Osvaldo snuggled into bed with a big smile on his face. He wasn't sad anymore. He felt safe, peaceful, and full of joy. Jesus was alive—and one day, Osvaldo would live forever with Him!

Questions:

1. Why did Jesus have to die?
2. What did Jesus say about life after we die?
3. How does it make Osvaldo feel to know Jesus is alive?
4. Why don't we need to be afraid of dying?

Practical Activity: Jump for Joy Resurrection Game

1. When you say "Jesus died," kids lie flat.
2. When you say, "Jesus rose!" they jump up and cheer!

LESSON 4: I AM A BOY MADE IN GOD'S IMAGE

Learning Objectives:

By the end of this lesson, children will be able to:

1. Understand that they are made in God's image and likeness, meaning they can think, imagine, and act in ways that reflect God's character.
2. Explain that being made in God's image means they are called to show kindness, wisdom, and strength, like the prince learning to be a good leader.
3. Identify qualities of good leadership and godly behavior, such as protecting others, doing what is right, and showing love.
4. Demonstrate a desire to imitate God's goodness and live according to His ways, through words, actions, or creative responses like drawing or role-playing.

Story: A Role Model

In a faraway kingdom, there lived a wise and kind king. One morning, he called his son, the prince. "I want to show you something," the king said. He took him for a walk around the kingdom and showed him green fields, sparkling rivers, busy towns, farmers planting, children playing, and guards keeping everyone safe. The king turned to him and said, "One day, this kingdom will be yours. But being a king is not just about wearing a crown. A real king leads with wisdom, kindness, and strength. He protects people and does what is right."

The prince said, "I want to be a good king like you, Daddy." The king smiled. "Then watch me, learn from me, and do what is right. That's how you become a great leader."

That night, the Prince remembered what his Sunday school teacher had told him from the Bible: **"The Son can do nothing of Himself, but what He sees the Father do."** *John 5:19. His teacher explained, "We were created in the very likeness and image of God, this means we are made to act like Him and use our imagination for good things."*

From that day on, the prince started following his dad everywhere to learn from him, just like Jesus followed His Father. He wanted to grow up to be a man who showed God's goodness, love, and strength.

Questions:

1. What did the king want to show his son?
2. What makes a real king, according to the story?
3. What does it mean to be made in God's image?
4. How can you be like God in your life?

Memory Verse

"Then God said, 'Let Us make man in Our image, according to Our likeness.'"
Genesis 1:26(NKJV)

SECTION 1: PART 1 - WHO AM I?
LESSON 4: I AM A BOY MADE IN GOD'S IMAGE

G126 MOVEMENT
BIBLE STUDY PROGRAM
FOR SUNDAY SCHOOL CHILDREN
AGES: 9-10 YEARS

 Activity: "A Kind Leader"

What you need: Paper and crayons or colored markers

What to do:

1. Draw a picture of yourself as a kind and wise leader.
2. Write or tell one way you can show kindness or help others this week.
3. Share your picture and idea with your family and practice being a good leader like the prince in the story!

Notes:

_____

_____

_____

_____

_____

LESSON 5: I AM A GIRL AND I AM SOMEONE SPECIAL

Learning Objectives:

By the end of this lesson, children will be able to:

1. Understand that girls and boys are both created in God's image, recognizing that both are equally important and loved.
2. Explain how God made the first woman, Eve.
3. Recognize their own value, beauty, and strength as a girl made by God's loving design.
4. Describe the meaning of walking "side by side" with others, promoting friendship, working together and respect for each other.

Story: Someone Special

A long time ago, the great and loving King made a beautiful world. He filled it with bright stars, tall trees, animals, flowers, and deep blue oceans. Then the King made a man from the dust of the ground. He breathed life into him, and the man became alive!

But something was missing. The man was strong and smart, but he was alone. So the King said, "It is not good for the man to be alone. I will make someone special just for him." The King caused the man to fall into a deep sleep and He took one of his ribs, and made a beautiful woman." Genesis 2:21

She was full of grace, beauty, and strength. She would be the man's partner and friend, working beside him with love and unity. When the man woke up and saw her, he was very happy to see someone like him.

God made both the man and the woman in His image. They were different, but both equally important and loved. The King made them to care for the world together. From that day on, they walked side by side, just as the King wanted. And every little girl after her—including you—is made with that same love, beauty, and strength.

Questions:

1. Who made the world and everything in it?
2. Why did God make the woman?
3. Where was the woman made from?
4. What makes you special?

Memory Verse

"So God created man in His own image; in the image of God He created him; male and female He created them."—Genesis 1:27(NKJV)

Activity: "Draw Your Special Self"

What you need: Paper and crayons or colored markers

What to do:

1. Draw a picture of yourself, showing what makes you special.
2. Write or tell one thing you love about being a girl.
3. Share your drawing with your family, and thank God for making you so special!

Notes:

_____
_____
_____
_____
_____

LESSON 6: I AM JUST LIKE MY HEAVENLY FATHER

Learning Objectives:

By the end of this lesson, children will be able to:

1. Understand that they are called to imitate God, like children copying their parents.
2. Identify qualities of God such as kindness, forgiveness, honesty and mercy, and see these good things in themselves when they act like God.
3. Describe ways they can show God's character in their daily actions, such as being kind, telling the truth, forgiving, and helping others.
4. Explain how they can be a "little picture" of God to others, through their behavior and their attitude.

Story: A Copy Puppy

One day, our family got a new female puppy to be a friend for our male dog. They loved each other right away! Soon, the female dog had a puppy of her own. When the puppy was born, it looked just like its dad-dog! It walked like him, it played like him, and even tilted its head the same funny way. We laughed and said, "It's like a little copy of his daddy!"

And you know what? We are like that puppy too! The Bible says: **"Be imitators of God as dear children."** Ephesians 5:1. This means we should try to be like God. Jesus loved people, He forgave others, He helped friends, and He told the truth.

The Bible tells us in Exodus 34:6, that: **"The Lord God is merciful and gracious, slow to anger, and abounding in mercy and truth."**

When we are kind, when we tell the truth, when we forgive, and when we help others, we show what God is like. We become a little picture of Him! Just like the puppy looks like its daddy, we can show the world God by the way we live.

Memory Verse

"Be imitators of God as dear children."
Ephesians 5:1 (NKJV)

Questions:

1. What did the puppy look like?
2. What does it mean to be an imitator of God?
3. What are some things Jesus did?
4. How can you show God to others?

Activity: "Copy Me" Game

1. One person is the "Leader," who makes simple moves like clapping his hands, stomping his feet, or smiling big.
2. Everyone else, "copies" the Leader exactly, just like the puppy copies its daddy!
3. Take turns being the Leader.
4. After playing Leader, talk about how we can copy God, by doing good things every day.

Notes:

LESSON 7: I FUNCTION LIKE MY HEAVENLY FATHER

Learning Objectives:

By the end of this lesson, children will be able to:

1. Understand that living like God, means showing kindness, showing mercy, and showing humility, by following God's example.

2. Explain why Paul chose to be kind, even to those who were mean to him, by recognizing God's kindness towards us.

3. Identify ways they can show God's love, through their actions at school and home; such as sharing, forgiving, and being gentle.

4. Recognize that they have the ability to live like God through His promises, becoming partakers of His divine nature (2 Peter 1:4).

5. Demonstrate kindness and mercy in their daily lives, influencing others positively through their example.

Story: Paul's Heart

Paul was a boy with a kind heart. Some kids at school were mean to him, and tried to make him sad. But Paul didn't get mad, or say mean things back. He stayed calm and smiled.

One day, Paul even shared his snack with a boy who had been mean to him before! Paul's friend asked, "Why are you still nice to him?" Paul said, "Because God is kind to me, even when I make mistakes. I want to be like God."

The Bible says: **"He has shown you, O man, what is good; and what does the Lord require of you but to do justly, to love mercy, and to walk humbly with your God?"**
Micah 6:8 (NKJV).

Because Paul was kind, the kids who were mean started to be nice too. When we are kind, we are like God!

Questions:

1. What did Paul do when kids were mean to him?
2. Why did Paul want to be kind?
3. What does Micah 6:8 tell us to do?
4. How did Paul's kindness change the other kids?

Activity: "Kindness Chain"

What you need: Paper strips, crayons, and sticky-tape or glue.

What to do:

1. Write or draw a kind action on a paper strip (like sharing, helping, saying "thank you").
2. Join the strips to make a paper chain.
3. Talk about how each kind act helps others, just like Paul's kindness helped his friends.
4. Hang your kindness chain where it can remind you to be kind every day!

Notes:

LESSON 8: I CAN IMAGINE

Learning Objectives:

By the end of this lesson, children will be able to:

1. Recognize that imagination is a gift from God, allowing them to think, dream, and create.
2. Explain that God gives them a "sound mind" to help them come up with ideas and solve problems.
3. Describe how faith and belief in God can help them follow their dreams, even when others don't understand their dreams.
4. Demonstrate perseverance by continuing to imagine and to learn, trusting that with God, all things are possible.
5. Express their own creative ideas through drawing, storytelling, or building something, reflecting their God-given imagination.

Story: Isaac's Imagination

Isaac was a boy with a BIG imagination. He liked to sit quietly and think. He thought about stars, new things and ways to help people.

One day, Isaac said to his mom, "I'm going to build a machine that helps people! Maybe it could clean up trash or carry heavy things for older people!"

His mom smiled and said, "That's a wonderful idea, Isaac! Big things start with ideas. By hard work and trusting God, your ideas can come true!"

Isaac's eyes brightened. He remembered a Bible verse from Sunday school: **"If you can believe, all things are possible to him who believes."** *Mark 9:23(NKJV)*

From that day on, Isaac started drawing pictures of machines. He also asked lots of questions about how things worked.

Even when others didn't understand or laughed at his ideas, Isaac didn't stop. He remembered another Bible verse: Isaac believed that God could use his imagination to create something helpful for people. So he kept dreaming, he kept learning, and he kept believing that anything was possible with God's help.

Questions:

1. What did Isaac like to do?
2. What was Isaac's idea?
3. What did Isaac's mom say about imagination?
4. What did the Bible verse say to Isaac?
5. What did Isaac do when people laughed at his ideas?

Activity: "Dream Machine"

What you need:

- Paper
- Crayons or colored markers
- Stickers (optional)

Instructions:

1. Give each child a piece of paper to draw on.
2. Ask them to think of a machine that can help people, just like Isaac. It could be a machine to clean up trash, or something to help carry heavy things, or even to make the world a better place.
3. Let them draw their idea and explain it to the class.
4. As they share their ideas, remind them that their imagination is a special gift from God, and by hard work. and their faith, they can make amazing things happen!

Memory Verse

"God has not given us a spirit of fear, but of power, love, and a sound mind."
2 Timothy 1:7(NKJV)

Notes:

LESSON 9: I AM A KING

Learning Objectives:

By the end of this lesson, children will be able to:

1. Understand that God chooses them to be part of His royal family, just like David was chosen to be king.

2. Explain that being a king means leading with love, courage, and wisdom; not just strength or size.

3. Find how David trusted God to face his fears and testes, and relate this to their own experiences with courage.

4. Describe how Jesus has made believers kings and priests in His Kingdom, empowering them to lead in God's ways.

Story: A King in the Making

There was a boy named David. He wasn't the tallest or the biggest. He didn't even fight in battles. He was just a young boy who took care of sheep. David loved God with all his heart.

One day, a giant, called Goliath, came to fight with God's people. Everyone was scared. The soldiers were too scared to fight him. But not David! David said, "The Lord will help me!"

David didn't have any armor or a big sword. All he had was a sling and a stone. But David trusted God. He wasn't scared, and he ran towards the giant. With God's help, David defeated Goliath!

God saw that David was brave and that he loved God with all his heart. Because of that, God chose David to be the king of His people—not because David was the strongest, but because David trusted God and because he followed God.

And guess what? God says you are chosen too! In the Bible, in 1 Peter 2:9, it says: **"You are a chosen people, a royal priesthood, to show others how good God is."** *So you are part of God's royal family! You may be young, but you are a king in the making. The Bible even says in Revelation 1:6 that Jesus has made us kings and priests—leaders in His Kingdom!*

So when you face something scary, like a big test or standing up for what's right, remember: God is with you, just like He was with David.

Questions:

1. What did David do for a living before he fought Goliath?
2. How did David fight Goliath?
3. Why did God choose David to be king?
4. What does the Bible say about you in 1 Peter 2:9?
5. How can you be a leader like David?

Activity: "A Royal Crown"

What you need:

- Yellow or gold paper
- Colored markers, stickers, glitter, or play-jewels
- Scissors (for teachers or helpers to cut)

Instructions:

1. Give each child a crown to decorate.
2. As they decorate, talk about how they are part of God's royal family, just like David.
3. When the crowns are finished, let the children wear them.
4. Remind them that they are kings and queens in the making, chosen by God.

Memory Verse

"You are a chosen people... a royal priesthood... to show others how good God is." — 1 Peter 2:9

Notes:

LESSON 10: I AM A QUEEN

Learning Objectives:

By the end of this lesson, children will be able to:

1. Know that being a queen, means showing bravery, kindness, and wisdom, just like Queen Esther.
2. Explain how Esther trusted God and prayed for help in a difficult time.
3. Describe how God can use them to do important and brave things, even if they feel scared.
4. Recognize the importance of helping others and standing up for what is right.
5. Demonstrate confidence in their own special strengths, and God's plan for their lives.

Story: Queen Esther

A long time ago, there was a girl called Esther. She didn't come from a rich family. She lived in a land called Persia. Esther lived with her cousin, Mordecai, who loved her very much. Esther loved God and always tried to be kind, gentle, and wise.

One day, the king of Persia wanted to find a new queen. Many girls were brought to the king, but when he saw Esther, he picked her! Esther became the queen of the whole land! But Esther had a secret—she was a Jewish girl, and no one knew.

Later, some bad people wanted to hurt all the Jewish people, and Esther was scared. But Mordecai reminded her, "Maybe, God made you a queen for this special time."

Esther prayed and asked God for help. Then, she did something very brave—she went to the king. The king could have been mad, but instead, he listened to Esther! Because of Esther's bravery, the king helped save the Jewish people. Esther wasn't just a queen because of her crown. She was a queen because she was brave and helped others. And you can be brave too!

God has made you special and strong, just like Esther. You can be brave, kind, and help others, too.

Questions:

1. Who was Esther's cousin?
2. What secret did Esther keep?
3. Why was Esther scared?
4. What did Mordecai say to Esther?
5. How did Esther show bravery?

Activity: "A Beautiful Crown"

What you need:

- Paper (yellow or gold)
- Colored markers, stickers, glitter
- Scissors (for teachers or helpers to cut)

Instructions:

1. Give each child a paper crown to decorate.
2. Ask them to color or decorate the crown however they like, and remind them that just like Esther, they are special and loved by God.
3. As they work, talk about how they can be brave and kind, just like Queen Esther.
4. Once they finish, let them wear the crowns and say: "I am brave, I am loved by God, and I can help others."

Notes:

LESSON 11: I AM CREATIVE LIKE MY FATHER

Learning Objectives:

By the end of this lesson, children will be able to:

1. Know that creativity is a special gift from God, given to help us make beautiful things.
2. Explain that God gave people talents like drawing, building, and creating so that we can honor Him.
3. Identify their own creative talents, and see these as a way to shine God's light.
4. Describe how they can use their creativity to make others happy and worship God.

Story: Pedro the Creative Boy

Pedro loved to draw, build, and think. One day, while painting a big rainbow with animals, he asked his daddy, "Daddy, where do ideas come from?" His daddy smiled and said, "Pedro, your creativity is a special gift from God! When you draw or when you build, you are using the talents God gave you. It shows a little bit of who He is."

"Really?" shouted Pedro, "Yes!" said his daddy. "A long time ago, God gave some people special talents to make a beautiful place for Him to live in and to meet with His people.

The Bible says, **'See, I have called by name Bezalel... and I have filled him with the Spirit of God, with wisdom, understanding, and skill to make beautiful things'** (Exodus 31:2-3).

His daddy read more from the Bible, "God gave them the ability to work with gold, silver, jewels, wood, and cloth to build the tabernacle — a very special place to worship God."

So God made artists and builders, just like me?" asked Pedro. "That's right," answered his daddy. "God gave you creative gifts to make others happy and to honor Him." Pedro smiled at his painting. "I want to keep drawing for God!"

His daddy said, "That's great, Pedro! Always do your best, because God gave you these gifts to shine His light." From that day, Pedro remembered that creativity is a gift from God, and he decided to use it for God Glory.

Questions:

1. What does Pedro like to do?
2. Who gave Pedro the gift to be creative?
3. What special talents did God give to Bezalel?
4. Why should we use our creativity?

Memory Verse

"Each of you should use whatever gift you have received to serve others."
1 Peter 4:10 (NIV)

Activity: Make Your Own Gift of Creativity!

What you need:

- Paper
- Crayons or colored markers
- Glue, stickers, or anything else you like to decorate things with

What to do:

1. Draw a picture of something you like to create. It could be a rainbow, an animal, a house, or anything you imagine!
2. Tell someone, "God gave me the gift to be creative!"
3. Show your picture to a family member and tell them what you learned about Pedro and creativity.

Notes:

LESSON 12: I AM BEING TRAINED: TO BECOME A MAN, A HUSBAND, AND A FATHER

Learning Objectives:

By the end of this lesson, children will be able to:

1. Know that becoming a man means learning to love, lead, and serve others, especially family.
2. Tell how biblical heroes like David and Daniel grew strong by following God and learning wisdom.
3. Know that Jesus grew in wisdom, strength, and favor with God and people as a model to follow.
4. Tell of the importance of a father's role in teaching, loving, and guiding his children according to God's ways.

Story: Leo and His Dad

Leo was a boy who loved spending time with his daddy. He always wondered how his dad managed to work so hard, and still have time for his family.

One day, Leo asked, "Daddy, Don't you get tired?" His dad smiled and said, "Leo, I do get tired. But being a real man is more than working or making money. It's about loving our family, leading by example, and following God. This is how I serve Him."

"Do you remember David?" his dad asked. Leo nodded, "He fought Goliath!" "Yes," his dad said. "But before he was king, David was a shepherd boy. He took care of sheep, played music, and spent time with God. The Bible says, **'So David went on and became great, and the Lord was with him'**" (1 Chronicles 11:9 -NKJV).

"We also have the example of Daniel and his friends," his Dad said. "They lived far from home, but stayed faithful to God. God gave them wisdom and helped them be leaders." His dad read, **"God gave them knowledge and skill in all learning and wisdom"** (Daniel 1:17 -NKJV).

Leo listened quietly to his dad. "And most of all," his dad said, "think about Jesus. When He was a boy, He obeyed His parents, and grew strong in wisdom. The Bible says, **'Jesus grew in wisdom and strength and in favor with God and people'**" (Luke 2:52).

His dad added, "When I do chores or pray with you, I'm showing love. The Bible says, **'If anyone does not provide for his relatives… he has denied the faith'**"
(1 Timothy 5:8 -ESV).

Leo's eyes got big. "So you're trying to be a leader like David and Daniel?" His dad laughed, "Yes, buddy, I have to follow Jesus' footsteps. As your dad, God wants me to raise you with love and patience, like Ephesians 6:4 says, **'Fathers, bring up your children in the training and instruction of the Lord.'**"

Leo hugged his dad tight. "I want to grow up like you—strong, wise, and full of love."

Questions:

1. What does it mean to be a real man, according to Leo's dad?
2. Who was David before he became king?
3. What did God give to Daniel and his friends?
4. How did Jesus grow when He was a boy?
5. What does Leo want to be when he grows up?

Memory Verse

"Be strong and courageous. Do not be afraid; do not be discouraged, for the Lord your God will be with you wherever you go." Joshua 1:9(NIV)

Activity: "My Family Helper"

What you need:

- A big sheet of paper or cardboard
- Colored markers or crayons
- Stickers or stars

What to do:

1. Draw a chart with 5 boxes.
2. Write labels for each box, with family jobs like: Help with chores, Be kind, Pray with family, Listen, and Help others.
3. Each day, try to do these jobs, and put a sticker or star in the box when you do it.
4. At the end of the week, talk with your family about how you are growing strong and loving like Jesus.

Notes:

LESSON 13: I AM BEING TRAINED: TO BECOME A WOMAN, A WIFE, AND A MOTHER

Learning Objectives:

By the end of this lesson, children will be able to:

1. Understand that God gives women special gifts to help and care for their families with love and joy.
2. Explain that doing small tasks, like cleaning and organizing, is important and pleasing to God when done with a happy heart.
3. Recognize that serving others at home is a way to show God's love and grow in wisdom and kindness.
4. Identify that learning to help at home now prepares girls to take care of their own homes in future.

Story: Lila and Her Mom

Everyday Lila watched her mommy work hard to make everything neat and peaceful at home. Her house always smelled warm and cozy.

"Mommy," Lila asked, "why do you clean and organize every day? Isn't it men's work?" Her mom smiled, and sat down with Lila. "God created me to be a helper to your dad," she said, "and I do it with joy. God made women with special gifts. The Bible says, **'It is not good for the man to be alone. I will make a helper suitable for him'"** *(Genesis 2:18).*

Lila looked around the house, and asked, "So, doing this, honors God?" Her mom nodded. "Yes! God cares about how we serve others, even in small things. The Bible says, **'Whatever you do, work at it with all your heart, as working for the Lord, not for people'"** (Colossians 3:23).

Her mom added, "One day you will have your own home. And you must be wise, kind, and loving, bringing joy to your family." She read from the Bible, **"She watches over the affairs of her household and does not eat the bread of idleness"** (Proverbs 31:27).

Lila smiled, and picked up her toys. "I want to start helping right now!"

Questions:

1. What special gift did God give to women?
2. What does it mean to be a helper?
3. How does working with love honor God?
4. What is one thing Lila wants to do after hearing the story?

Activity: "Helping Hands"

What you need:

- Paper
- Crayons or colored markers
- Scissors (with adult help)
- Glue or sticky-tape

What to do:

1. Trace your hand on a piece of paper.
2. Then, cut out the hand you drew on the paper.
3. On each finger, write or draw one way you can help your family (like cleaning, being kind, praying, sharing toys, …).
4. Decorate your "Helping Hand" with colors and stickers.
5. Share your Helping Hand with your family and tell them how you want to serve with love.

Notes:

LESSON 14: I AM CREATED TO BRING LIFE AND BE PRODUCTIVE

Learning Objectives:

By the end of this lesson, children will be able to:

1. Understand that God created us to bring life, and do good things to help other people.
2. Explain that using our gifts and talents, is like planting seeds that grow and help people.
3. Recognize that staying close to Jesus, helps us grow and be productive.
4. Identify ways they can be productive, like helping family, being kind, or learning new things.

Story: Colorful Backyard

One sunny afternoon, Laura went to visit her grandma in the village. As soon as she arrived, she ran to the backyard to see the garden. "Wow!" she gasped. "So many colors!" Grandma's garden was full of life. There were big, healthy plants—lettuce, tomatoes, green peppers, onions, chilies, and even some fruit.

The vegetables looked bright and fresh, because Grandma took very good care of them. "Your garden is so beautiful, and full of life, Grandma!" Laura said.

Grandma smiled, and handed her a small watering can. "Come," she said. "Let me show you something special." They walked between rows of tomatoes, carrots, and tall sunflowers. "Laura," Grandma said, "did you know that God created us to bring life—just like this garden?"

Laura looked curious. "What do you mean?" Grandma sat beside a tomato plant. "Every gift God gives us," Grandma said, "is like a seed. When we take care of it, it grows and helps others. Just like I plant seeds in the soil, God plants dreams, talents, and kindness inside of you."

She smiled and added, "When you help your mom, when you are kind to a friend, or when you learn something new, you are being productive. You are using the gifts God gave you."

The bible says in John 15:5 **"I am the vine, you are the branches. He who abides in Me, and I in him, bears much fruit; for without Me you can do nothing."** (NKJV)

"See?" said Grandma. "When we stay close to Jesus, He helps us grow. We can do amazing things with His help." Laura looked around the garden and whispered, "I want to grow good fruit too, Grandma."

Questions:

1. What did Laura see in Grandma's garden?
2. What did Grandma say gifts from God are like?
3. How can we be productive?
4. Who helps us grow good fruit?

Memory Verse

"Let all that you do be done with love." — 1 Corinthians 16:14 (NKJV)

Activity: A Seed of Kindness

What you need:

- Small plant pot or cup
- Soil
- Seeds (flower or vegetable seeds)
- Water

What to do:

1. Fill the pot with soil.
2. Plant a seed carefully in the soil.
3. Water the seed and place it where it can get sunlight.
4. Take care of your seed every day and watch it grow.
5. While waiting, think of ways you can grow kindness and good things in your heart, just like the plant grows.

SECTION 1: PART 1 - WHO AM I?
LESSON 14: I AM CREATED TO BRING LIFE AND BE PRODUCTIVE

Notes:

LESSON 15: I AM CREATED TO CONCEIVE AND GIVE BIRTH TO GOD'S PURPOSE ON THE EARTH

Learning Objectives:

By the end of this lesson, children will be able to:

1. Understand that God's purpose for the Earth is to bring His Kingdom here, full of love, peace, truth, and goodness.
2. Explain that living like Jesus means loving others, helping people, and telling the truth.
3. Recognize that even small acts of kindness and prayer help bring God's Kingdom to Earth.
4. Describe how saying "yes" to God, means listening and doing what He wants every day.

Story: Bringing God's Kingdom to Earth

Anna was reading her Sunday school notebook. She saw something very important written there: "God's purpose for the Earth is to bring His Kingdom here, just like it is in Heaven."

So, she wondered, "How can I help bring God's Kingdom to Earth?" She closed her notebook, and went to find her mom, who was sitting with a cup of tea. "Mommy," Anna asked, "how can I help God bring His Kingdom here on Earth?"

Her mom smiled and put down her cup. "That's a wonderful question, Anna. God's Kingdom is full of love, peace, truth, and goodness. When we live like Jesus taught us—by loving others, helping people, and telling the truth—we are bringing God's Kingdom to Earth."

Anna tilted her head. "So, even the little things I do matter?" "Yes," her mom said. "Every kind word, every prayer, every good thing you do helps. God has put His special purpose inside you. It's like a tiny seed. When you use your gifts to help others, that seed grows big and strong."

Mom opened the Bible and read: **"And Mary said, 'Behold the maidservant of the Lord! Let it be to me according to your word.'"** (Luke 1:38 -NKJV)

"Just like Mary said 'yes' to God's plan," her mom said, "you can say 'yes' too—by listening to God, and doing what He wants every day, even in little ways."

That night, Anna wrote in her notebook: "I can bring God's Kingdom to Earth by living like Jesus."

Questions:

1. What did Anna want to know?
2. What is God's Kingdom full of?
3. How can we bring God's Kingdom to Earth?
4. What did Mary say to God?
5. What did Anna decide to do?

Activity: "Yes to Jesus"

What you need:

- Red or pink paper
- Scissors (with help)
- Crayons or colored markers
- Stickers or decorations (optional)

What to do:

1. Cut out a big heart from the paper.
2. Write or draw things you can say "yes" to Jesus about—like being kind, praying, helping, or telling the truth.
3. Decorate your heart with colors and stickers.
4. Put your "Yes to Jesus" heart somewhere you can see it every day to remind you to live like Jesus.

Notes:

LESSON 16: I AM BEAUTIFUL IN MY SPIRIT, MY SOUL, AND MY BODY

Learning Objectives:

By the end of this lesson, children will be able to:

1. Name our three parts that God made us: spirit, soul, and body.

2. Understand that our body is what we see and feel, our soul is our mind and feelings, and our spirit is the part that talks with God.

3. Explain that sometimes these parts can feel like they don't agree, but they all work together to make us who we are.

4. Recognize that growing strong in spirit by praying, reading the Bible, and learning God's truth helps us make good choices.

5. Express that God made us beautiful, and He wants us to take care of our spirit, our soul, and our body.

Story: Inner Battle

One day, Carolina sat on her bed, looking worried. She was confused, because she wanted to do something; but, inside her, part of her said "yes" and part of her said "no." She didn't know why she felt this way.

Her dad walked by, saw her and he asked, "Carolina, are you okay? What's wrong?" Carolina looked up. "I feel like I'm having a war inside me! One part wants to do something, but another part says no."

Her dad smiled and sat down next to her. "That's something everyone feels sometimes. We all have three parts: a spirit, a soul, and a body. Sometimes they just don't agree." Carolina asked, "Why does this happen?" Her dad explained, "Your body is what you see and feel. It is comfortable and fun. Your soul is your mind and feelings—how you think and what you want. Your spirit is the deepest part inside of you—it's the part that talks with God."

He read from the Bible: **"Now may the God of peace Himself sanctify you completely; and may your whole spirit, soul, and body be preserved blameless at the coming of our Lord Jesus Christ."**
(1 Thessalonians 5:23 -NKJV)

"You are beautiful, not just because of how you look, but because God made you with a spirit, a soul, and a body—all working together. When your spirit is strong and close to God, it helps your soul and body make good choices." Said her dad.

"Wow," Carolina said. "So, my feelings and thoughts were real, but I can learn to listen more to my spirit?" "Yes!" Dad smiled. "When you spend time praying, reading the Bible, and learning God's truth, your spirit grows strong. It helps you do what is right—even when it's hard."

Carolina gave her dad a big hug. "Thanks, Daddy! I want to grow strong in all three—my spirit, my soul, and my body!"

Questions:

1. What was Carolina feeling inside?

2. What are the three God gave us?
3. What does your spirit do?
4. What does the Bible say about your spirit, your soul, and you body?
5. How can we make our spirit strong?

Activity: "Spirit, Soul, and Body"

What you need:

- Paper
- Crayons or colored markers
- Scissors (with help)

What to do:

1. Draw a big heart
2. Divide it into three parts.
3. Label one part "Spirit," one part "Soul," and one part "Body."
4. In each part, draw or write something that helps that part grow strong.
  ★ For Spirit: praying, talking to God, reading the Bible
  ★ For Soul: thinking good thoughts, being kind, feeling happy
  ★ For Body: eating healthy, playing, resting
5. Color your heart
6. Hang your heart where you can see it every day, to remember to take care of all three parts.

Notes:

LESSON 17: I AM AN ORIGINAL

Learning Objectives:

By the end of this lesson, children will be able to:

1. Understand that God made each person special and unique, with their own gifts and their own purpose.
2. Recognize that God did not make mistakes when creating them—they are wonderfully made.
3. Express joy and confidence by saying, "I am not a copy. I am an original."
4. Begin to think about their own special gifts and talents.

Knowledge Text: The Special Me

Did you know that God gave every person a special job to do? Each of us has different gifts to help us do it in our own way. So, never compare yourself to others—because God made you original and unique! Think about fingerprints. No two people have the same fingerprints—not even twins who look just alike! Even their fingerprints are different. You are not ordinary. You are one of a kind!

God made you with a special purpose that no one else can do like you can.

The Bible says: **"I will praise you, for I am fearfully and wonderfully made; Marvelous are Your works, And that my soul knows very well."**
Psalm 139:14(NKJV)

God didn't make a mistake when He made you, He gave you your smile, your voice, your thoughts, and your heart on purpose.

If you don't know your special gift yet, that's okay! You'll discover it as you grow up. So, every time you look in the mirror, say to yourself with joy: "I am not a copy. I am an original. I am God's special creation."

Questions:

1. What makes you different from everyone else?
2. Why must you never compare yourself to others?
3. What are fingerprints? Why are they special?
4. What does the Bible say about how we are made?
5. What can you say to yourself when you look in the mirror?

Activity: "My Unique Gift"

What you need:

- Paper
- Crayons or colored markers
- Stickers (optional)

What to do:

1. Draw a big picture of yourself in the middle of the paper.
2. Around your picture, write or draw things that make you special—like your smile, your favorite hobby, or something you're good at doing.

3. Decorate your poster with colors and stickers.
4. Hang your poster up to remind yourself that you are an original and God's special creation!

Notes:

LESSON 18: I SPEAK LIKE MY HEAVENLY FATHER

Learning Objectives:

By the end of this lesson, children will be able to:

1. Understand that words have power—my words can hurt or my words can help others.
2. Recognize that God wants us to use kind and loving words like He does.
3. Explain why speaking kindly is important to show love and care.
4. Identify examples of kind words they can say to others, like "Thank you," "I'm proud of you," and "You did a great job."
5. Choose to use kind words instead of teasing or saying mean things.

Story: Clemence's Words Matter

Clemence loved to play and laugh with his friends and his little brother, Nathan. But sometimes, Clemence teased Nathan a lot. He called him silly names and made fun of him when Nathan made mistakes. Nathan looked sad, but Clemence didn't think much about it.

One day, Clemence was at his friend's house. He heard his friend's dad say, "Words are powerful. Words can help people or words can hurt them. God made the whole world by speaking words!

He wants us to speak like Him—using words to bless, to heal, and to help other people." Clemence listened carefully.

That night, he thought, "My words can hurt or my words can help." He suddenly remembered what his Sunday School teacher said: **"Death and life are in the power of the tongue, And those who love it will eat its fruit."**
Proverbs 18:21(NKJV)

Clemence felt sorry. He thought about the times he made his brother cry.

The next morning, when Nathan dropped his spoon, Clemence smiled and said, "It's okay! I'll help you clean it up." Nathan was surprised, but happy. From that day, Clemence chose to stop teasing. Rather, he used kind words, like, "You did a great job!" "Thank you for sharing!" "I'm proud of you!"

Every time Clemence spoke kindly, he felt happy inside. And Nathan smiled more and more.

Questions:

1. What kind of words did Clemence say to Nathan before?
2. Why are words powerful?
3. What did Clemence decide to do with his words?
4. How do kind words make people feel?
5. What does the Bible say about the power of words?

Memory Verse

"Death and life are in the power of the tongue, And those who love it will eat its fruit." Proverbs 18:21(NKJV)

Activity: "Kind Words Tree"

What you need:

- Paper
- Crayons or colored markers
- Scissors (with help)

What to do:

1. Draw a big tree with lots of branches on paper.
2. Cut out small paper leaves or use colored paper.
3. On each leaf, write a kind word or phrase you can say to help others (like "Thank you," "Great job," or "I'm proud of you!")
4. Glue or tape the leaves onto the tree branches.
5. Hang your Kind Words Tree where you can see it, to remind you to use kind words every day!

SECTION 1: PART 1 - WHO AM I?
LESSON 18: I SPEAK LIKE MY HEAVENLY FATHER

Notes:

LESSON 19: I AM LOVED BY MY HEAVENLY FATHER

Learning Objectives:

By the end of this lesson, children will be able to:

1. Understand that everyone makes sometimes mistakes, and that's okay.
2. Know that God loves them, no matter what, even when they mess up.
3. Retell the story of the lost son, and how the father welcomed him back with love.
4. Recognize that God is like the father in the story—always ready to forgive us and love us.
5. Feel comforted and safe, knowing that God's love is unconditional and never-ending.

Story: Duarte's Nightmare

Duarte was a boy who liked helping at home, and tried to be good. But, sometimes, he made mistakes—like forgetting to clean up, getting upset with his little sister, or talking back.

One day, he asked his mom, "Mommy, will you still love me if I mess up?" His mom hugged him, and said, "I love you no matter what. Even if you make mistakes, I will always be your mom, and I will always love you."

Duarte smiled, but still wondered if God could love him no matter what. At Sunday School that week, Duarte's teacher told a story from the Bible. It was about a boy who made big mistakes but whose father still loved him very much.

She read Luke 15:11-32, the story Jesus told about a man who had two sons. The younger son asked for his share of the money and left home. He spent all the money on wrong things, and ended up with nothing—not even food! He had to feed pigs and was so hungry he wanted to eat their food!

Finally, the son said, "I will go home and tell my father I'm sorry. Maybe he will let me work for him." But, when the father saw his son coming, he didn't get mad. He ran to him, hugged him tight, and threw a big party; because his son had come home. The father said, "My son was lost, but now he is found!"

Duarte's eyes got big. His teacher said, "That's how God loves you. Even when you mess up, God never stops loving you. He is always ready to welcome you back." That night, Duarte whispered, "My mom loves me no matter what... and God loves me even more." He smiled, and thanked God for His love.

Memory Verse

"But God demonstrates His own love toward us, in that while we were still sinners, Christ died for us."
Romans 5:8 (NKJV)

Questions:

1. What did Duarte wonder about love?
2. What did the younger son do in the Bible story?
3. How did the father react when his son came back?
4. What does this story tell us about God's love?

Activity: "God's love Never Fails"

What you need: Red and white paper, scissors, crayons, glue.

What to do:

1. Cut out a big red heart
2. Then, cut out a smaller white heart.
3. On the red heart, write or draw something you love about God or your family.
4. On the white heart, write or draw a time you felt loved even when you made a mistake.
5. Glue the white heart on top of the red heart.
6. Talk about how God's love is bigger, and always covers our mistakes.

Notes:

PART TWO
Why am I Here?

LESSON 20: I AM CREATED IN GOD'S IMAGE AND LIKENESS

Learning Objectives:

By the end of this lesson, children will be able to:

1. Explain what it means to be created in God's image and likeness.
2. Identify key qualities of God (such as love, creativity, power, and forgiveness) that are seen in human beings.
3. Describe how having the "mind of Christ" enables them to think, imagine, and act in positive ways.
4. Recognize the importance of keeping good and kind thoughts about themselves and others.
5. Express how being made in God's image makes each person special, and how it encourages them to live a loving and creative life.

Knowledge Text

In Genesis 1:26-27, it is written in the Bible: **"Let Us make man in Our image, according to Our likeness."** *What does this mean? Does God look like us, with two feet and two hands? Not really! God is a Spirit, but when He made us, He put a little bit of Himself inside us. This means:*

- *God is very smart, and He gave us a mind to think and learn. The Bible says in 1 Corinthians 2:16 that* **"But we have the mind of Christ." Therefore we can think and imagine good things like God.**
- God is full of love, and He wants us to love others too. God is kind and caring, and we can be kind to our friends and care for our family.
- God is powerful, He can do anything! And He gives us strength to do good things.
- God can forgive us when we make mistakes, and He wants us to forgive others too.
- God is creative, He made the whole world! and He made us creative as well. We can draw, sing, and make new things, just like God.
- God lives forever, and if we believe in Jesus, we will live forever too!

But, we have to be careful about the way we think. The Bible says in Proverbs 4:23: **"Keep your heart with all diligence, For out of it spring the issues of life."**

This means, we should think good and kind thoughts about ourselves and how we must also think of other people.

Questions:

1. What does Genesis 1:26-27 say about how we were made?
2. What special gift did God give us, according to 1 Corinthians 2:16?
3. Why does Proverbs 4:23 tell us to watch our thoughts?
4. How can you show love and kindness to others like God?

Activity: "Made in God's Image Collage"

What you need:

- Paper
- Crayons, colored markers, or colored pencils
- Magazines or printed pictures (optional)
- Glue or sticky-tape

Instructions:

1. Draw a big picture of yourself in the middle of the paper.
2. Around your picture, draw or paste pictures that show how you are like God. For example:

★ a heart for love

★ a light bulb for thinking

★ hands helping for kindness, or

★ a smile for forgiveness.

3. Talk about your pictures and how these show that you are made in God's image.

Notes:

LESSON 21: I AM CREATED TO HAVE DOMINION

Learning Objectives:

By the end of this lesson, children will be able to:

1. Explain the meaning of having dominion over the earth as described in Genesis 1:26; and what responsibilities this dominion includes.

2. Describe the roles God has given human beings to be leaders and caretakers of animals, plants, and the environment.

3. Understand the important place of human beings in God's creation.

4. Identify ways they can responsibly care for and protect God's creation in their daily lives.

Comprehension Text:

God made you for a very special reason. When a company makes a toy or a game, they write down what it is for—its purpose. God did the same thing when He made you!

The Bible says in Genesis 1:26(NKJV): **"Let Us make man in Our image, according to Our likeness; let them have dominion over the fish of the sea, over the birds of the air, and over the cattle, over all the earth and over every creeping thing that creeps on the earth."**

This means, God gave you a job to do, to have dominion and take care of the world He made as a leader! But, being a leader, doesn't mean bossing others around. Being a leader means being responsible and caring. You get to take care of the animals, plants, and everything God put on the earth.

King David was amazed that God made people rulers over everything. Psalm 8:6 says **God has made Man to have dominion over the works of His hands; He has put all things under his feet!"**

God made you important and gave you a big job to do! You must rule the earth for God, and look after the treasures and gifts God put on the earth.

Memory Verse

Genesis 1:26 "Let Us make man in Our image, according to Our likeness; let them have dominion..."(NKJV)

Questions:

1. What does Genesis 1:26 say God gave us?
2. What does it mean to have dominion over the earth?
3. How can you take care of God's creation?
4. What did King David say about how God made human beings? (Psalm 8:6)

Activity: "My Dominion Park"

What you need:

- Paper
- Crayons or colored markers
- Stickers or pictures of animals and plants (optional)

Instructions:

1. Draw a park land where you are the caretaker.
2. Draw animals, trees, flowers, and rivers that you will take care of.
3. Write or say one way you will take care of each thing in your drawing.
4. Talk about why you need to be responsible and kind to God's creation.

Notes:

LESSON 22: MY PURPOSE IS CONNECTED TO THE EARTH

Learning Objectives:

By the end of this lesson, children will be able to:

1. Describe how God created fish, birds, and human beings.
2. Explain why human beings were made from the dust of the earth.
3. Recognize that being a part of earth, God gives human beings a unique purpose related to caring for the world.
4. Identify ways they can take care of God's creation. and appreciate the natural world around them.
5. Express why they are special, because they are created to live in harmony with both the earth and God's spirit.

Comprehension Text:

When God made the fish, He spoke to the waters. The Bible says in Genesis 1:20: **"Let the waters bring forth abundantly the moving creature that has life..."** *God told the fish to come forth, out of the water!*

Then, He spoke to the sky, and said, **"Let birds fly in the sky!"**

So, every creature is connected to where it came from—fish belong in water, birds belong in the sky.

When God made people, it was very special. The Bible says in Genesis 2:7(NKJV): **"And the Lord God formed man of the dust of the ground, and breathed into his nostrils the breath of life; and man became a living being."**

God took part of the earth—dust from the ground—and made our bodies. Then God breathed His own spirit into us. That means we are part of earth and part of God!

Because our bodies come from the earth, our purpose is connected to the earth too. We live here to take care of God's creation, and enjoy the world He made.

You are special, made by God to live in this beautiful world!

Questions:

1. What did God tell the waters to do in Genesis 1:20?
2. What two parts did God use to make man, according to Genesis 2:7?
3. Why are we connected to the earth?
4. How can we take care of the earth God gave us?

 ## Activity: "A Mixture of Earth and Heaven"

What you need:

- Two sheets of paper or one divided into two halves
- Crayons, colored markers, or colored pencils
- Cotton balls or blue tissue paper (for sky/heaven)
- Dirt or brown paper pieces (for earth)

Instructions:

1. On one paper half, draw or glue things from the earth like trees, animals, flowers, and soil.
2. On the other half, draw or glue things from the sky or heaven, like clouds, sun, stars, and angels.
3. Talk about how you are made from both parts—earth and heaven—and why that makes you special!

Notes:

LESSON 23: I AM A MANAGER AND INFLUENCER

Learning Objectives:

By the end of this lesson, children will be able to:

1. Explain the story of the faithful servant from Luke 12:42–44, and its lesson about responsibility and faithfulness.
2. Describe how God gave Adam and us the role of managers to take care of the earth and everything in it.
3. Identify their own gifts, and how these can be used to serve others; rather than to brag or control.
4. Understand how their good actions reflect God's love.
5. Demonstrate ways they can be good managers and positive influencers in their homes, communities, and environment.

Comprehension Text:

Jesus told a story in Luke 12:42–44 about a good servant, who took care of his master's house. When the master saw the servant doing a great job, he gave him even more important things to do! This shows God wants us to be faithful and responsible.

God gave each of us special gifts, not so we can brag or boss others around; but so we can help and serve.

In Genesis 1:15, God put Adam in the Garden of Eden to take care of it. That means Adam was the manager of God's garden!

Just like Adam, God wants us to take care of everything around us, our homes, nature, and the people we love. We are managers of the earth! Even though some people think the earth is crowded, there is still so much that needs our care and help.

Jesus said in Matthew 5:13-16 that we are like salt and light: **"You are the salt of the earth... You are the light of the world. Let your light shine before men, that they may see your good works and glorify your Father in heaven."**

This means when we do good things, we can influence others, and help them see God's love.

Memory Verse

Luke 12:42 "Who then is that faithful and wise steward, whom his master will make ruler over his household, to give them their portion of food in due season?"(NKJV)

Questions:

1. What did the master do when he saw the servant taking care of the house?
2. What job did God give Adam in Genesis 1:15?
3. What does Jesus say we are like in Matthew 5:13-16?
4. How can you be a good manager and help other people?

Activity: "Let Your Light Shine!"

What you need:

- A paper-plate or circle cut from paper
- Yellow, orange, and white crayons or markers
- Stickers or glitter (optional)

Instructions:

1. Color the paper circle bright yellow and orange like the sun.
2. Write or draw one good thing you can do to shine God's light this week (like helping a friend, sharing, or being kind).
3. Decorate your sun with stickers or glitter to make it shine!
4. Hang your sun somewhere to remind you to be a good manager and light for God.

Notes:

LESSON 24: I AM A BUILDER AND REPAIRER

Learning Objectives:

By the end of this lesson, children will be able to:

1. Explain the meaning of being a "repairer of the breach" using Isaiah 58:12.

2. Describe how Nehemiah took action to rebuild the broken walls of Jerusalem, and why that was important.

3. Identify different ways they can help repair things that are broken, including friendships and feelings.

4. Understand the importance of being proactive in helping others, and making situations better.

5. Demonstrate how loving and helping others, can bring healing and hope to their communities.

Comprehension Text:

The Bible says in Isaiah 58:12b(NKJV) **"You shall be called the Repairer of the Breach."**

God wants us to help fix things that are broken. Sometimes things get broken like walls or houses.

Sometimes it's feelings or friendships that get hurt. God calls us to be helpers who fix and make things better.

In Nehemiah 2:17-18, Nehemiah saw the walls around Jerusalem were broken and falling down. Instead of waiting for someone else to fix them, he started rebuilding the walls himself!

God wants us to be like Nehemiah — builders and repairers wherever we go. We can help fix broken friendships, we can make others feel happy again, and we can bring hope to people who are sad.

When we love and when we help others, we bring healing and we make the world a better place for everyone.

Questions:

1. What does Isaiah 58:12 say God wants us to do?
2. What did Nehemiah do when he saw the broken walls?
3. How can you be a builder and repairer at home or at school?
4. Why is it important to help fix broken things or friendships?

Activity: "The Repairer!"

What you need:

- Paper
- Crayons or colored markers
- Scissors
- Sticky-tape or glue

Instructions:

1. Draw a big broken heart or a broken wall on paper with cracks.
2. Cut out little paper "patches" (shapes like hearts or squares).
3. Color and decorate the patches.
4. Glue or tape the patches over the cracks to fix the heart or wall.
5. Talk about how God wants us to fix things and help others feel better.

Notes:

LESSON 25: I AM CALLED TO LEAD

Learning Objectives:

By the end of this lesson, children will be able to:

1. Describe the qualities of a good leader, emphasizing kindness, fairness, and servant leadership modeled by Jesus.
2. Identify different places and ways they can practice leadership in their own lives, such as at school, home, and community.
3. Understand the impact of righteous leadership on people's well-being.
4. Express the importance of striving to be a leader, who brings joy, peace, and safety to others.

Comprehension Text:

From the very start, God gave people the job of taking care of the earth. That means we are all called to be rulers—not by being bossy, but by being kind, fair, and leading like Jesus.

In Genesis 1:28, God said to Adam: ***"Be fruitful and multiply; fill the earth and subdue it; have dominion over the fish of the sea, over the birds of the air, and over every living thing."***

Adam was told to take care of the earth, and we have the same job today!

We can be leaders at school, at home, in our neighborhoods, and even in big jobs when we grow up, like president, mayor, or governor.

The Bible says in Proverbs 29:2(NKJV) **"When the righteous are in authority, the people rejoice; But when the wicked rule, the people groan."** Meaning, when good people lead, everyone is happy and safe. When bad people lead, things get very hard.

God wants you and me to be good leaders who bring joy and peace wherever we go!

Questions:

1. What job did God give Adam to do in Genesis 1:28?
2. What does it mean to lead like Jesus?
3. What happens when good people lead, according to Proverbs 29:2?
4. How can you be a good leader at home or school?

 Activity: "The Great Leader"

What you need:

- Paper or card stock
- Crayons, colored markers, or stickers
- Scissors
- Sticky-tape or glue

Instructions:

1. Cut a long strip of paper to fit around your head, to make a crown.
2. Decorate your crown with colors, stickers, or drawings.
3. Write or draw one way you will be a good leader this week on your crown.
4. When you wear your crown, remember that God calls you to lead with kindness and love!

Notes:

LESSON 26: I CAN SUBDUE AND OVERCOME

Learning Objectives:

By the end of this lesson, children will be able to:

1. Explain the meaning of "subdue," and how subduing applies to overcoming challenges and difficulties.

2. Identify common struggles such as fear, bad thoughts, or external problems; and how to face these with God's help.

3. Recite and say the key Bible verse means about overcoming evil and finding strength in Christ (Romans 12:21).

4. Describe ways to respond with good and right actions when faced with negative situations or feelings.

Comprehension Text:

God made you strong! That means you can win against things that try to stop you from doing what God wants. The word "subdue" means to make something obey even when it's hard to do that. Sometimes we have problems like storms or sickness. Sometimes we feel scared, or we have bad thoughts like "I'm not good enough." But guess what? You can overcome all of that!

When bad things try to pull you down—like anger, fear, or someone being mean, you can choose to do good and right things with God's help.

The Bible also says in Philippians 4:13(NKJV): **"I can do all things through Christ who strengthens me."** And 2 Timothy 1:7(NKJV), it says **"For God has not given us a spirit of fear, but of power and of love and of a sound mind."**

When you feel scared or think bad thoughts, remember: God made you strong, full of His power, and you can win!

Memory Verse

Romans 12:21 "Do not be overcome by evil, but overcome evil with good."
(NKJV)

Questions:

1. What does it mean to "subdue" something?
2. What does Romans 12:21 tell us to do when bad things try to win?
3. How does Philippians 4:13 help you when you feel weak or scared?
4. What kind of spirit does God give us, according to 2 Timothy 1:7?

Activity: "The Super Shield"

What you need:

- Paper plate or card stock
- Colored markers, crayons, or stickers
- Popsicle stick or straw (for a handle)
- Sticky-tape or glue

Instructions:

1. Decorate your paper plate or card stock like a shield.
2. Write the memory verse or words like "Strong," "Brave," and "God's Power" on it.
3. Tape or glue a handle (Popsicle stick or straw) on the back to hold your shield.
4. Use your shield to remind yourself that God gives you power to overcome anything!

Notes:

LESSON 27: I AM CALLED TO EXCEL AND GROW

Learning Objectives:

By the end of this lesson, children will be able to:

1. Explain why God wants us to grow and improve, comparing this to a good father's desire for his children.
2. Describe ways they can grow in love, kindness, wisdom, and leadership—by following God's example.
3. Identify practical steps to grow spiritually, such as learning from God's Word and following Jesus daily.
4. Explain how Jesus' growth is as a model for their own development.

Knowledge Text:

Many kids grow up to do what their parents do, like becoming teachers, builders, or helpers.

In the same way, we are God's children, and He wants us to do what He does—like showing love, helping others, leading with kindness, and growing in wisdom.

To grow, we need to learn new things, listen to God's Word, and follow Jesus every day. Growing doesn't just happen by itself—we have to choose to grow in how we think, how we act, and how much we know God.

The Bible teaches us in Luke 2:52 that Jesus increased in wisdom and stature and found favor before God and men. God wants us to grow and get better, just like a good father wants his children to grow strong and wise.

Questions:

1. What does God want us to do, like Jesus did, according to Luke 2:52?
2. How can you grow every day?
3. What does 2 Peter 3:18 tell us to grow in?
4. Why is it important to learn more about God?

Activity: "Growing with Jesus"

What you need:

- Paper
- Crayons or colored markers
- Stickers or cut-out leaves (optional)

Instructions:

1. Draw a big tree trunk and branches on your paper.
2. Each day this week, write or draw one way you will grow closer to God (like praying, reading the Bible, being kind).
3. Add a leaf or sticker to your tree for each way you grow.
4. Watch your tree grow full of leaves, just like you grow in God's love!

Notes:

LESSON 28: I CAN BE PRODUCTIVE AND FRUITFUL

Learning Objectives:

By the end of this lesson, children will be able to:

1. Explain the meaning of being fruitful and productive according to Genesis 1:28.

2. Identify their unique talents, gifts, or ideas that God has given them to use for good.

3. Describe how using their minds, time, and abilities can help others and make a positive impact.

4. Understand the meaning of having "the mind of Christ" (1 Corinthians 2:16) in thinking wisely and creatively.

5. Demonstrate ways to be productive and fruitful in their daily lives, by applying their talents and gifts.

Comprehension Text:

Did you know the very first thing God told people to do was to be fruitful? That means God wants us to grow, create, and make good things with our lives!

In Genesis 1:28, God said: **"Be fruitful and multiply, and fill the earth and subdue it!"** *God wants us to grow and use everything He gave us—our minds, time, talents, and hearts—to do good things. Jesus picked you to do special things that help other people and last a long time!*

You have something special inside you—a talent, an idea, or a gift—that God wants to grow. Some people don't use what God gave them, but you can!

The Bible says in 1 Corinthians 2:16 that you have the mind of Christ. This means you can think wisely, you can create, and you can be productive.

Memory Verse

John 15:16 "I have chosen you and appointed you, that you should go and bear fruit, and that your fruit should remain."(NKJV)

Questions:

1. What did God tell us to do in Genesis 1:28?
2. What does Jesus say in John 15:16 about the job He gave us?
3. What special thing do we have inside us, according to 1 Corinthians 2:16?
4. How can you be productive and use what God gave you?

Activity: " Be productive and fruitful "

What you need:

- Paper or card stock
- Crayons or colored markers
- Paper cut-out fruit shapes (or you can draw fruit)
- Glue or sticky-tape

Instructions:

1. Draw or cut out a tree trunk with branches on paper.
2. Color or draw fruit on paper, or use precut fruit shapes.
3. On each fruit, write or draw one good thing you can do or create using your talents (like helping, sharing, singing).
4. Glue or tape the fruit onto the tree branches.
5. Display your fruit tree as a reminder to be productive and fruitful for God.

Notes:

LESSON 29: I AM HERE TO BUILD AND BRING BACK

Learning Objectives:

By the end of this lesson, children will be able to:

1. Explain how being created in God's image includes the ability to build, establish, and restore.
2. Describe the importance of starting new helpful things and fixing what is broken in their communities.
3. Identify feelings that arise when projects or goals are not yet finished, and how to respond with perseverance.
4. Understand their role in working with God to improve homes, schools, communities, and churches.
5. Share ideas for how they can start new projects or help others who are making a difference to their worlds.

Comprehension Text:

God made you to build and fix things! That is part of His image in you. Just like God made and took care of the earth in the beginning, you have the power to create, start new things, and fix what is broken. Sometimes people feel sad or frustrated when they can't finish something important. That is because God made us want to do good and make a difference to things around us!

But, instead of just being upset when things go wrong, God wants us to help make things better. So you can work with God to build up and fix broken homes, fix broken schools, fix broken communities, and fix broken churches.

Maybe you will start something new someday, like a business or a helping group, or you can help support other people who do good work.

Memory Verse

John 3:17 "For God did not send His Son into the world to condemn the world, but that the world through Him might be saved."(NKJV)

Questions:

1. What does God want you to do with things that are broken?
2. What does John 3:17 tell us about Jesus' job?
3. What are some things you can help fix or build?
4. Why is it good to help other people who are doing good work?

Activity: "Rebuild "

What you need:

- Building blocks or paper and crayons
- Paper and colored markers

Instructions:

1. Build something with blocks—a house, a school, or anything you like.
2. Take apart your building.
3. Then try to fix it, or build it better.
4. Talk about how sometimes things get broken, but we can always restore or fix them.
5. Draw a picture of something you want to build, or help restore to make the world better!

Notes:

LESSON 30: I HAVE GIFTS AND TALENTS

Learning Objectives:

By the end of this lesson, children will be able to:

1. Describe how God gave Moses special gifts to help him lead and do miracles.
2. Identify their own gifts and talents, whether natural abilities or spiritual gifts from the Holy Spirit.
3. Tell of the importance of using their gifts to help other people, and to fulfill God's purpose for them.
4. Understand the story of the man who buried his talent in the ground, and why God wants us to use our gifts to make more (Matthew 25:29).
5. Show confidence in sharing and growing their gifts, trusting that God will give them more opportunities.

Comprehension Text:

A long time ago, God chose Moses to do a very important job—to lead His people out of slavery in Egypt.

At first, Moses felt scared and not ready. He was shy and unsure of himself. But, God had given Moses special gifts to help him. God gave Moses the power to do miracles and lead many people. Moses used those gifts to do what God wanted him to do! Exodus 4:10-12.

Just like Moses, you also have gifts and talents from God. Maybe you are good at drawing, or singing, or playing sports. Maybe you are good at praying for others or you are good at telling stories. Some gifts you are born with, and some come from the Holy Spirit as you grow.

Sometimes people are afraid to use their gifts. There is a story in the Bible about a man who buried his one talent in the ground, because he was scared. But, God wants us to use our gifts to help other people and grow.

The Bible says in Matthew 25:29a(NKJV): "**For to everyone who has, more will be given.**" This means the more you use your gifts, the more God will trust you with even more!

Questions:

1. How did Moses feel when God asked him to lead?
2. What kinds of gifts can God give you?
3. What does the story about the talents teach us?
4. Why is it good to use the gifts God gives you?

Activity: "My Gift Container"

What you need:

- Small box or paper bag
- Paper and crayons or colored markers
- Stickers (optional)

Instructions:

1. Decorate a box or bag to look special—this is your "Gift Container."
2. Draw or write down some of your talents and gifts on small pieces of paper.
3. Put those papers inside your gift container.
4. Each day, take one gift out of your gift container.
5. Then, think of one way you can use your gift to help other people, or help them grow!

Notes:

LESSON 31: I AM A PROBLEM SOLVER

Learning Objectives:

By the end of this lesson, children will be able to:

1. Explain how God created each child with unique gifts and special ability to help solve problems in the world.
2. Identify examples of problem solvers in the Bible and from everyday life, including Jesus and Joseph.
3. Recognize problems they care about, and that they feel called to help fix in their own communities.
4. Understand the importance of trusting God for guidance in solving problems.
5. Demonstrate confidence in their ability to make a difference to their world never mind their age or size.

Knowledge Text:

God made you special with your own gifts, talents, and ideas because He knew the world would need someone just like you to help solve problems. Think about some big problem solvers:

- *Jesus solved the biggest problem ever—sin!*
- *Joseph in the Bible. He helped solve the problem of no food in Egypt.*
- *People like Bill Gates, who solved problems with computers.*
- *Cars help people go quickly where they need to be.*
- *Clothes help keep us warm and covered up.*

Guess what? You were born to solve a problem too! Maybe you care about animals or plants, helping other people, or protecting nature. When something makes you feel upset or worried, that might be God's way of telling you to help fix it.

The Bible says in John 3:17(NKJV) **"For God did not send His Son into the world to condemn the world, but that the world through Him might be saved."** *Jesus came to fix the biggest problem!*

Proverbs 3:5-6(NKJV) says **"Trust in the Lord with all your heart, and lean not on your own understanding; in all your ways acknowledge Him, and He shall direct your paths."**

When you trust God, He will help you solve problems. When you solve problems for other people, it shows how awesome and good God is! So never think you are too young or too small to make a difference to your world.

Memory Verse

Proverbs 3:5 "Trust in the Lord with all your heart, and lean not on your own understanding."(NKJV)

Questions:

1. Who is the biggest problem solver?
2. What are some ways people solve problems?
3. How can you tell God wants you to help solve a problem?
4. Why should you never think you're too small to help?

Activity: "A young Detective"

What you need:

- Paper and crayons or colored markers
- A list of simple everyday problems (like a messy room, a sad friend, broken toy)

Instructions:

1. Think of a problem you see around you or have known about.
2. Draw a picture of the problem.
3. Now, draw a picture of how you could help fix it or how you can solve it!
4. Share your drawings and ideas with family or friends.

Notes:

LESSON 32: I AM FEARLESS

Learning Objectives:

By the end of this lesson, children will be able to:

1. Identify common fears that can stop people from following God's plan.

2. Explain the meaning of 2 Timothy 1:7, and how God gives us power, love, and a sound mind, instead of fear.

3. Using Psalm 56:3 from the Bible, describe how trusting God helps overcome fear.

4. Recognize that God is a loving Father Who wants to help them grow, and not punish them for their mistakes.

Knowledge Text:

Being scared is the number one thing that stops people from doing what God wants them to do! God has amazing plans for you—plans that need faith and courage. But sometimes, fear tries to whisper things like:

- *"You're not good enough."*
- *"What if you fail?"*
- *"What if people laugh at you?"*

God says something very different in 2 Timothy 1:7 (NKJV): **"For God has not given us a spirit of fear, but of power and of love and of a sound mind."**

God wants you to trust Him and not be scared. He's not waiting to punish you if you make a mistake. He's a kind and loving Father Who wants to help you learn and grow. When you stop being afraid, a whole new world of exciting things to do, opens up for you. You can do what God has called you to do!

The Bible also says in Psalm 56:3(NKJV) **"Whenever I am afraid, I will trust in You."**

So when you feel scared, remember to trust God!

Questions:

1. What does fear try to tell us?
2. What does God say about the spirit He gave us?
3. What can you do when you feel afraid?
4. Why does God want us to be with no fear at all?

Activity: "I am a Superhero"

What you need:

- Paper and crayons or colored markers
- Optional: stickers or glitter

Instructions:

1. Draw yourself as a superhero, who is brave/bold.
2. On your superhero cape or outfit, write or draw the words "Power," "Love," and "Self-control."

3. Think of one thing you are afraid of.
4. When you are scared, say a prayer, asking God to help you to be brave.

Notes:

LESSON 33: I AM PART OF A BIGGER PICTURE

Learning Objectives:

By the end of this lesson, children will be able to:

1. Explain how each person is like a unique piece of a big puzzle (1 Corinthians 12:12).
2. Describe how everyone has a special place and job within the family of God, and also in their community.
3. Understand the importance of working together, sharing, helping, and loving other people rather than only thinking about themselves all the time.
4. Recognize that problems in families and communities can help us grow stronger.

Knowledge Text:

Imagine a big puzzle. Every piece is different, but each piece is very important to make the whole picture complete. God made each of us like a living stone, special and unique. He wants us to work together like one big family we call the Body of Christ.

Just like in your own family, everyone has a special job to do. Sometimes families have problems, but problems don't break the family! They help us learn to be stronger and kinder.

When we only think about ourselves, we forget how important it is to care for other. People too. God wants us to think about our family, our friends, and our community, to share, help, and love one another.

The Bible says in 1 Corinthians 12:12(NKJV) **"For as the body is one and has many members, but all the members of that one body, being many, are one body, so also is Christ."**

So, even though we are all different, we belong together, and we all need each other!

Memory Verse

Romans 12:5 "So we, being many, are one body in Christ, and individually members of one another."(NKJV)

Questions:

1. What is the big puzzle like?
2. Why does God want us to work together?
3. What happens when families have problems?
4. How can you help your family and friends?

Activity: "The Big Puzzle"

What you need:

- Paper
- Crayons or colored markers
- Scissors

Instructions:

1. Draw or trace a big puzzle piece on a piece of paper.
2. Decorate your puzzle piece with your name and pictures of things you love or ways you help others.
3. Cut out your puzzle piece.
4. Fit your puzzle piece with all the puzzle pieces made by your family or friends, to show how you all fit together!

Notes:

LESSON 34: I MAKE A DIFFERENCE

Learning Objectives:

By the end of this lesson, children will be able to:

1. Explain the purpose God has for them to make a difference on earth, not just wait to go to heaven someday.
2. Identify ways their hands, talents, and gifts can be used to help other people and glorify God.
3. Understand the importance of finding and using their gifts to do good works, based on Ephesians 2:10.
4. Express a commitment to working with God to restore joy, peace, and hope in the world.

Knowledge Text:

The people in the Bible knew why God made them. Their goal wasn't just to go to heaven later someday—they wanted to make a difference here on earth while they lived. God gave you hands and talents so that you can do amazing things! Your hands can create, they can help other people, they can build, and your hands can even do miracles when you use them for God's kingdom.

Sometimes we don't use our gifts because we don't know how yet. But when we find out what God wants us to do, and start using our gifts, we can make a big difference for God's glory!

The Bible says in Ephesians 2:10 (NKJV) **"For we are His workmanship, created in Christ Jesus for good works, which God prepared beforehand that we should walk in them."** God made you do good things!

Let's work together to take back what the enemy tries to steal—like joy, peace, and hope—and honor God, by doing His will here on earth, just like it is in heaven.

Memory Verse

Matthew 5:16 "Let your light so shine before men, that they may see your good works and glorify your Father in heaven."(NKJV)

Questions:

1. What did people in the Bible want to do here on earth?
2. What can your hands do for God?
3. Why do some people not use their gifts?
4. How can you make a difference for God?

Activity: "Shine for God"

What you need:

- A paper lantern or a simple paper cut-out of a light bulb
- Crayons, colored markers, or stickers

Instructions:

1. Color and decorate your lantern or light bulb with things that show how you can make a difference (like helping, sharing, praying).
2. Hang it somewhere you can see it every day to remind you to shine your light for God!
3. Share one good thing you can do this week to help other people.

Notes:

LESSON 35: I NEED WISDOM AND HELP

Learning Objectives:

By the end of this lesson, children will be able to:

1. Describe who King Solomon was and why God's wisdom is important for happiness and success.

2. Understand the role of the Holy Spirit as our Helper Who guides and Who teaches us (John 14:26).

3. Recognize the importance of asking the Holy Spirit for help when we are facing difficult decisions or challenges.

4. Demonstrate how to seek God's wisdom and guidance in their daily lives through their prayer and their trust in Him.

Comprehension Text:

King Solomon was the wisest and richest man in the Bible. Did you know that your happiness and success come from how much wisdom you have? God wants us to use the wisdom He gives to make good choices, to plan for things, and to build things that help us live well.

The Bible says in Proverbs 1:7(NKJV) **"The fear of the Lord is the beginning of knowledge, but fools despise wisdom and instruction."**

When we respect God and trust Him, we begin to be wise too.

When you need help, God's Spirit is right beside you! Jesus called Him the Helper, the Holy Spirit. But He won't help unless you ask Him to help you. So, when you feel stuck, just say, "Holy Spirit, please help me," and He will guide you in the right way for you.

In John 14:26(NKJV) it says **"But the Helper, the Holy Spirit, whom the Father will send in My name, He will teach you all things."** Just ask!

Questions:

1. Who was the wisest man in the Bible?
2. What does "fear of the Lord" mean?
3. Who is the Helper Jesus talked about?
4. What can you say when you need help?

Activity: "Our Helper"

What you need:

- Paper and crayons or colored markers
- A small "help" sign or card

Instructions:

1. Draw a picture of King Solomon.
2. Make a "Help Me!" card to carry with you.
3. Write the verse John 14:26 on the back of your card
4. When you need help, or you want to make a good choice, look at your card, and then read the verse on the back of it.
5. Then say, "Holy Spirit, please help me!"

Notes:

LESSON 36: I AM A BLESSING

Learning Objectives:

By the end of this lesson, children will be able to:

1. Explain what it means to be a blessing to other people, using the fruit tree idea.
2. Describe how God blesses us, so we can bless other people too.
3. Understand the need of waiting and trust in God, while we waiting for His blessings to grow bigger.
4. Explain the meaning of Acts 20:35, about the joy and value of giving more than receiving.
5. Demonstrate ways they can be a blessing, by sharing, helping, and encouraging other people every day.

Comprehension Text:

Think about a fruit tree:

- *First, you plant a little fruit seed.*
- *The seed grows deep in the right ground.*
- *The tree grows bigger, and makes fruit.*
- *The fruit has seeds that can grow into more fruit trees.*

The tree doesn't grow fruit just for itself. It grows fruit to bless other people too! God wants us to be like that tree. To help other people to learn and to grow, we need to be a blessing to them first.

Genesis 12:2(NKJV) says **"I will make you a great nation; I will bless you and make your name great, and you shall be a blessing."**

Also, Jesus said in Acts 20:35b(NKJV): **"It is more blessed to give than to receive."**

When we share and help, we bring God's blessings to others too!

It takes time for the tree to grow and bear fruit, so we need to be patient and trust in God, as we wait.

Questions:

1. What does it mean to be a blessing?
2. What are the steps a seed takes to grow into a fruit tree?
3. Why does a tree make fruit?
4. How can you be a blessing to other people?

Activity: "Seed of Blessings"

What you need:

- Paper and crayons
- A small pot or cup
- Soil and a seed (like a bean seed)

Instructions:

1. Draw a picture of a fruit tree or a seed growing.

2. Plant your seed in the pot.
3. Take care of the seed, by watering it a little bit.
4. Then, watch it grow week after week.
5. Talk about how your seed will grow and bless other people by making fruit one day.
6. Talk about how just like the fruit of a seed, you too can be a blessing, by helping other people!

Notes:

LESSON 37: I PROTECT AND CARE FOR

Learning Objectives:

By the end of this lesson, children will be able to:

1. Explain that the earth belongs to God, but He has given it to us to care for and protect for Him.
2. Describe why taking care of the earth is important.
3. Identify ways God gave us the job to look after and keep the earth.
4. Understand that caring for the environment is a special job given by God to all His children today.
5. Demonstrate practical ways they can protect and care for the earth in their daily lives.

Comprehension Text:

God gave us a very special gift—the whole earth! Everything we need to live comes from the earth: the food we eat, the water we drink, and the air we breathe.

Heaven belongs to God, but He gave the earth to us, His children. So, it's our job to take care of the earth and keep it safe for everybody just like you take care of all your toys.

Think about your family car—if your dad doesn't take care of it, it might break down or stop working. But, if he keeps it clean, and he fixes it when it's broken, it will last for a long time to come.

God gave Adam the job of caring for the garden. That was a big, important job! We have the same job today, to protect God's creation, and care for the earth.

Memory Verse

Genesis 2:15 "And the Lord God took the man and put him in the garden of Eden to tend and keep it."(NKJV)

Questions:

1. What did God give us to take care of?
2. Why is it important to keep the earth safe for everyone?
3. What did God ask Adam to do?
4. How can you help take care of the earth?

Activity: "Earth Care Champion"

What you need:

- Paper and crayons
- A small trash bag or box

Instructions:

1. Draw a picture of the earth.

2. Talk about ways you can help take care of the earth (like picking up trash, saving water, planting flowers).
3. Go on a mini clean-up walk with a friend, and pick up any litter you see lying on the ground, to take good care of the earth!

Notes:

LESSON 38: I REBUILD RELATIONSHIPS

Learning Objectives:

By the end of this lesson, children will be able to:

1. Understand the importance of having close, loving friendships with your family and your friends.
2. Describe how broken relationships can make life hard for everybody, and why rebuilding them matters.
3. Talk about Romans 12:18 about living peacefully with others as much as possible.
4. Explain Jesus' command to love God and love others people (Matthew 22:37-39), and how love helps to build strong relationships.

Comprehension Text:

God made you His special child! Who you really are, comes from your relationship with Him. It does not come from how you look. It does not come from what you do. And. It does not come from where you come from.

We have our body from our parents, but our spirit—the real you—comes from God. When we don't feel close to God, we may feel empty or sad inside.

God also made us have close friendships with our family and our friends. When our relationships are not good, life feels hard and not happy at all.

The Bible says in Romans 12:18(NKJV) to us, is: **"If it is possible, as much as depends on you, live peacefully with all men."**

God's most important command is to love Him with all our heart, and to love other people just like we love ourselves. When we love God and love other people, our relationships grow strong and happy!

Memory Verse

Matthew 22:37-39 "You shall love the Lord your God with all your heart... and your neighbor as yourself."(NKJV)

Questions:

1. Where does your true worth come from?
2. What can happen when we don't have good relationships?
3. What does the Bible say we should do with other people?
4. How can you show love to your family and your friends?

Activity: "A Friendship Bridge"

What you need:

- Paper and crayons
- Popsicle sticks or paper strips (optional)

Instructions:

1. Draw a picture of you on one piece of paper.
2. On a new piece of paper, draw a friend or your family.
3. Then, draw a bridge of hearts on it, to show love and peace.
4. Talk about ways you can build bridges—like saying sorry, like sharing, like helping, or like giving hugs to fix or grow relationships.

Notes:

LESSON 39: I AM CREATED TO RULE IN MY AREA

Learning Objectives:

By the end of this lesson, children will be able to:

1. Understand that God created each person with unique gifts and a special purpose.
2. Describe how David's experiences caring for sheep helped prepare him for greater leadership.
3. Recognize the importance of practicing and growing their own gifts to serve and lead other people.
4. Identify ways they can use their unique talents to lead and help other people in their own place where God put them.

Comprehension Text:

The Bible says in 1 Corinthians 12:4-5(NKJV) **"There are diversities of gifts, but the same Spirit. There are differences in ministries, but the same Lord."**

God made every person special with a purpose. Everyone's purpose is special But how you do your purpose is different because God gave you one of a kind gifts.

One good example is David. He was a shepherd boy who took care of sheep. But David also practiced playing music, and he learnt to be brave.

One day, David met the king. And because of his gifts, David got a very big chance to help the kind and to lead his people!

In 1 Samuel 17:34-37, David says how God helped him protect his sheep from lions and bears. This made David strong, and made him ready for bigger things.

God wants you to use and grow your gifts too. When you do this, you will be able to lead and help others in your own special way too.

Questions:

1. What makes your gifts and purpose different from other people's gifts and their purpose?
2. What job did David do before he became a leader?
3. How did David use his gifts?
4. How can you use your gifts?

Activity: Special Flowers"

What you need:

- Paper and crayons
- Stickers or small craft items

Instructions:

1. Draw a garden with flowers.
2. Write or draw one special gift God gave you on each flower.
3. Talk about how you can use and grow these gifts to help other people!

Notes:

LESSON 40: I REPRESENT GOD'S KINGDOM

Learning Objectives:

By the end of this lesson, children will be able to:

1. Explain how God's creation, like the stars and sky, reveals His greatness.
2. Describe how Jesus showed God's glory through His actions of kindness, healing, and love.
3. Understand the role of Ambassadors for Christ, representing God's kingdom on earth.
4. Identify ways they can show God's love and kingdom through their own words and their own actions.
5. Recognize the importance of living like Jesus so others can see God's kingdom through their lives.

Knowledge Text:

Everything God made shows us how amazing He is? The stars, the sky, the earth, and even YOU, show how amazing God is!

The Bible says in Psalm 19:1(NKJV) **"The heavens declare the glory of God; and the firmament shows His handiwork."** *This means, when we look at the sky and stars, we can see how great God is!*

Jesus showed God's glory, by doing wonderful things. He helped people. He healed the sick, and He loved everyone. When people saw Jesus, they saw God's kindness and power.

Now, Jesus wants us to represent God's kingdom. That means when we do good things, like forgiving, being kind, helping other peoples, and telling the truth—people can see God's love in us.

God sent Jesus to save us, and bring His kingdom to earth. Because of this, the Bible says in 2 Corinthians 5:20 (NKJV) **"Now then, we are ambassadors for Christ, as though God were pleading through us: we implore you on Christ's behalf, be reconciled to God."**

An ambassador is someone who represents a king or country. You are God's ambassador, so when you live like Jesus, you show God's kingdom to the world!

Questions:

1. What does Psalm 19:1 say about the sky and stars?
2. How did Jesus show God's glory?
3. What does it mean to represent God's kingdom?
4. How can you be an ambassador for Jesus?

Activity: "Kingdom Ambassador Badge"

What you need:

- Paper or card stock
- Crayons, colored markers, or stickers
- Safety pin or sticky-tape

Instructions:

1. Draw a badge or shield shape on the paper.
2. Write "Kingdom's Ambassador" on it.
3. Decorate it with colors and stickers.
4. Stick a safety pin or sticky-tape on the back of it
5. Then, wear it like a real ambassador!
6. Every day, remember you represent God's kingdom by doing good and loving other people.

Notes:

LESSON 41: CREATION IS WAITING FOR ME

Learning Objectives:

By the end of this lesson, children will be able to:

1. Talk about what sin did to creation, and why the world needs Jesus to fix it.
2. Describe what it means that creation is waiting for God's children to be revealed.
3. Understand their job as being "salt and light" in the world.
4. Identify practical ways to show God's love and truth in their daily actions.

Knowledge Text:

A long time ago, Adam did not listen to God. Because of that, the whole world, all the plants, all the animals, and all the people fell short of God Glory.

But, because of God's love, Jesus came to fix everything! He did this by dying on the cross, and rising up from the dead again. Now, He wants us to help finish the work of making the world good again too.

The Bible says in Romans 8:19 **"The creation waits in eager expectation for the children of God to be revealed."**

This means all of creation, all the plants, all the animals, and all people are waiting for God's children, like you, to come and show God's love and God's truth.

No matter what job you have when you grow up, be it a doctor, teacher, or just a parent, God wants you to show Jesus to the world. You can do this by being kind, by loving others, and by telling the truth.

In Matthew 5:13-16(NKJV), Jesus said **"You are the salt of the earth... You are the light of the world... Let your light shine before men, that they may see your good works and glorify your Father in heaven."**

So, we don't have to shout, or scare people, but we can be like salt and light, helping and shining by how we act every day. When people see us loving others, they can see God's glory in us!

Questions:

1. What happened when Adam disobeyed God?
2. How did Jesus help fix the world?
3. What does Romans 8:19 tell us about creation?
4. How can we be like salt and light to others?

Activity: Sunshine

What you need:

- Paper plate or card stock
- Yellow and orange crayons or colored markers
- Glue and glitter (optional)
- String or ribbon

Instructions:

1. Draw a big sun or light rays on the paper plate or card stock.
2. Color it bright yellow and orange to look like the sun is shining.
3. Add glitter if you want to make it sparkle!
4. Make a hole in it, and tie a string to it, so you can hang it somewhere you'll see it every day.
5. Remember, just like your sunlight card shines, you can shine Jesus' love to everyone around you too!

Notes:

PART THREE

Where did I come from?

LESSON 42: I COME FROM GOD

Learning Objectives:

By the end of this lesson, children will be able to:

1. Say that God is the Creator of everything, including people, animals, plants, the sky, and the sea.
2. Describe how Adam was made from dust, and made alive by God's breath.
3. Talk about ways that people are made to be like God, such as loving other people, helping them, creating things, and leading people.
4. Explain the meaning of Genesis 2:7 in their own words, showing they know that Life comes from God.

Comprehension Text:

God is the Creator of everything! He made the whole world, He made the sky, He made the sea, He made the animals, and He made every plant.

After making all of these things, God decided to make people, too. He wanted people to live on the Earth, and take care of it. He made us to be like Him. That means, we can do things that God does—like loving other people, like creating new things, like helping, and like leading people.

The very first person God made was a man called Adam. God made Adam's body out of dust from the ground, but Adam wasn't alive yet. He needed God's special gift. God breathed His own breath into Adam, and when He did, Adam came alive! God's breath was very special—it was the spirit of God, which made Adam into a living person.

Did you know that we are all made like Adam? We are alive, because God gave us His breath, too! That means you have something very special inside of you, God's own breath. You come from God, and are made to be like Him.

Questions:

1. What did God make before He made people?
2. How did God make Adam come alive?
3. What is special about you and me?
4. How can we show God's love to other people?

Memory Verse

"Then the LORD God formed man of the dust of the ground, and breathed into his nostrils the breath of life; and man became a living being."
Genesis 2:7 (NKJV)

 ### Activity: God's Creation Craft

Supplies:

- Let's make a God's Creation Craft!
- You will need paper, crayons, or colored markers.

Instructions:

1. Draw a picture of yourself in the center, because God made you live in His beautiful Earth.
2. Then, draw the trees, animals, ... on your picture of the Earth.
3. On the back of your drawing, write or ask a parent to write: "I am made in God's image!"
4. Show your picture to your family.
5. Tell your family what you learned—God made you special, and you come from Him.

Notes:

LESSON 43: I COME FROM HEAVEN

Learning Objectives:

By the end of this lesson, children will be able to:

1. Know that they are chosen by God, and that they are not here by accident.
2. Explain that they came from Heaven, and were sent to Earth for a special job.
3. Describe ways they can show God's love and kindness, such as being kind, forgiving, sharing, and telling the truth.
4. Recognize that they can be God's voice on Earth, acting as His hands and His feet, by doing good and speaking kindly.
5. Say that God trusts them and He values them, and they can feel confident that they are important in God's big plan for the world.

Knowledge Text:

You were in God before you were born. He made you for a very special reason and sent you to Earth at just the right time—right now! God sent you here to show His love, to show His kindness, and to show His light to the world.

This means you're not here by chance; God chose you! Every time you do something kind, every time you forgive someone, every time share your toys, or you tell the truth—you are sharing in building God's Kingdom on Earth.

You are very needed to God. You are His hands, you are His feet, and you are His voice here on Earth. If God wants to help someone, He can use you. If God wants to say something to someone, He may say it through you!

You have access to Heaven through God Spirit, and everything you see in Heaven, you can so do the same here on Earth.

Wow! You are a gift from Heaven! Everywhere you go, you carry God's love and God's light. Keep shining bright!

Questions:

1. Where were you before you were born?
2. Why did God send you to Earth?
3. What are some ways you can show God's love?
4. How can you help bring God's Kingdom to Earth?
5. What does it mean to be God's hands, God's feet, and God's voice?

Memory Verse

"Your Kingdom come. Your will be done on earth as it is in heaven." Matthew 6:10(NKJV)

Activity: Mission Trip

Supplies: Paper, crayons or colored markers

Instructions:

1. Draw a picture of yourself standing on Earth.
2. Also draw around your picture, some hearts, light, and kind things—like sharing, helping, or praying.
3. Write (or ask a grown-up to write) this sentence at the top: *"God sent me from Heaven to share His light on Earth!"*
4. Hang you that you are on a special mission from Heaven to Earth!

Notes:

LESSON 44: I COME FROM THE KINGDOM OF HEAVEN

Learning Objectives:

By the end of this lesson, children will be able to:

1. Understand that they are part of God's Kingdom when they accept Jesus and are born again.
2. Explain that they are royal messengers of God on Earth, and must share His love, kindness, and truth.
3. Describe what it means to be "born again", in simple terms such as "joining God's family" and "becoming part of His Kingdom."
4. Recognize that to pray to believe and to obey are like using God's powerful keys to bring good changes to the world.
5. Be sure that they come from the God's Kingdom.

Comprehension Text:

A Long time ago, God decided to create Earth. This was because He wanted His Heavenly Kingdom to grow!

When we believe in Jesus, and choose to follow Him, something amazing will happen someday through His Word. We will see His Kingdom, and will be born again into it. From that very moment, we are children of the Kingdom of Heaven.

Jesus said the Kingdom of Heaven gives us wonderful keys! These keys are not for doors, but for making good changes on Earth. When we pray, believe, and follow God's ways, we are using those keys to help others find the Kingdom. And that is how we make the world a better place to live in.

Even though we live here, on Earth, we come from the Kingdom of Heaven. so, God needs us to make His Kingdom bigger here on Earth, by bringing His love and goodness into every aspect of life!

Questions:

1. What does it mean to be "born again?"
2. What kingdom do we belong to, when we are born again?
3. What kind of job does God give us, here on Earth?
4. What are the "keys" Jesus gave us, used for?
5. How can you share God's love with other people today?

Memory Verse

"Jesus answered and said to him, 'Most assuredly, I say to you, unless one is born again, he cannot see the kingdom of God.'" John 3:3(NKJV)

Activity: Keys for God's Kingdom

Supplies: Paper, scissors, crayons or colored markers

Instructions:

1. Draw 3 big "keys" on paper.
2. Then, cut out the 3 keys.
3. On each key, write (or let someone help you write) one way you can use your "Kingdom keys:"
★ Key 1: Pray for someone
★ Key 2: Forgive someone
★ Key 3: Tell the truth
4. Decorate your keys with bright colors and hearts!
5. Hang your keys on a wall or your fridge, to remind you that:
★ You have the power to make the world a better place!

Notes:

LESSON 45: I AM A KINGDOM AMBASSADOR

Learning Objectives:

By the end of this lesson, children will be able to:

1. Know what an ambassador is, and tell how they show their home (God's Kingdom) here on Earth.
2. Recognize that they are Kingdom Ambassadors, chosen by God to show others what His Kingdom is like.
3. Identify ways they can represent God, like showing love, showing kindness, showing peace, and showing truth to other people.
4. Explain that part of their special job as ambassadors, is telling other people about Jesus.
5. Tell, that part of their special job as ambassadors, is to tell others people about living the Kingdom way.

Knowledge Text:

An ambassador is a person who live in a different place, and who talks and acts for their home country.

For example, if someone is from Mozambique, but goes to live in another country, so, they can tell those other people about Mozambique; and show how people there live.

The same for when you are born again, you become a Kingdom Ambassador! That means, you represent God's Kingdom here on Earth.

You must show other people what our King is like, and show how life in the Kingdom is; show the Kingdom culture, show the entertainment, show the media, show Kingdom farming, show Kingdom learning, show Kingdom government, and show Kingdom health.

When a kingdom sends an ambassador, they want to bring their own way of life to a new place. That is what we do for God's Kingdom—we bring God's peace, we bring God's love, we bring God's truth, and we bring God's light to everyone around us!

So, you are God's special ambassador! Wherever you go, you show His love and you show His kindness to everyone you meet. You are helping to bring God's Kingdom to Earth!

Questions:

1. What is an ambassador?
2. Who do you represent as a Kingdom Ambassador?
3. What kind of things does God want you to share with other people?
4. How do we bring God's Kingdom to the world?
5. Can you think of one way to be kind or loving this week?

SECTION 1: PART 3 - WHERE DID I COME FROM?

LESSON 45: I AM A KINGDOM AMBASSADOR

G126 MOVEMENT
BIBLE STUDY PROGRAM
FOR SUNDAY SCHOOL CHILDREN
AGES: 9-10 YEARS

Memory Verse

"We are therefore Christ's ambassadors, as though God were making his appeal through us."
2 Corinthians 5:20(NKJV)

Activity: The Kingdom Ambassador!

Supplies: Paper, crayons or colored markers, scissors, sticky-tape or safety pins

Instructions:

1. Draw a big round circle on paper to make a badge.
2. Write "Kingdom Ambassador" in the middle of your circle.
3. Draw hearts, crosses, or anything on your circle to remind you of God's love for you.
4. Color your badge bright and happy!
5. Cut it out.
6. Ask an adult to help tape or pin it to your shirt.
7. Wear your badge to remind you that you represent God everywhere you go!

Notes:

http://www.Treeof-life.com

© TREE OF LIFE

LESSON 46: I AM MADE/CREATED BY GOD ALMIGHTY

Learning Objectives:

By the end of this lesson, children will be able to:

1. Understand that every part of who they are, was made by God with His love and care.
2. Recognize that they are unique and special, with gifts, talents, and a job that only they can do for God.
3. List some of the special gifts or talents God t gives, such as helping people, drawing, speaking kindly, or leading other people.
4. Tell that there is no need to compare people because God made everyone different for a special reason.
5. Feel confident and thankful for how God made them, knowing they are wonderfully made by God Almighty.

Comprehension Text:

God is the best artist in the whole world He made you! He took special time to create every part of you! He made your smile, He made your voice, He made your mind, and your personality—was made on purpose by God Himself.

God made you long before you were even inside your mommy's tummy. He didn't make any mistakes. You are perfect and God gave you a special job too, something only you can do!

Maybe you are good at helping other people, good at drawing pictures, good at speaking kindly, good at solving puzzles, or good at leading your friends. All those things you are good at doing, are gifts God gave to you to do.

Sometimes, we feel bad when we compare ourselves to others. But, that is like comparing the day and the night, or light and darkness; or simply comparing a dress and a bag! Both a dress and a bag are important, but they each do different things! God made you, to be you, with gifts only you have; and that is wonderful!

Questions:

1. Who made you?
2. Did God make any mistakes, when He made you?
3. What are some special things God gave you?
4. Why shouldn't we compare ourselves to other people?
5. What is something special that you are good at doing?

Memory Verse

"For You formed my inward parts; You covered me in my mother's womb." Psalm 139:13 (NKJV)

Activity: God made Me Special

Supplies: Paper, magazines or printed pictures, glue, crayons or colored markers

Instructions:

1. Cut out pictures of things you like or things you are good at doing (like animals, toys, art supplies, friends, …).
2. Glue the pictures on your paper to make a collage that shows how God made you special.
3. Write or add a big title at the top, that says: "God Made Me Special!"
4. Color and decorate your collage with bright colors.
5. Share your collage with your family, and tell them what makes you special!

Notes:

LESSON 47: I AM SKILFULLY AND WONDERFULLY MADE

Learning Objectives:

By the end of this lesson, children will be able to:

1. Understand that God made every part of them on purpose, with great care and skill .

2. Recognize that their hands and their talents can be used to do good things, like helping people, creating things, and learning new things.

3. Explain the idea of "potential" in simple words knowing they have special abilities inside them that can grow through doing them again and again.

4. Identify ways they can do their best—at home, in school, and with other people—because this honors God, and shows His greatness.

Comprehension Text:

God made every part of you with His great skill and care. He did not just put you together quickly—He made you like a master artist! From your fingers to your brain, from your heart to your smile—all of you was wonderfully made by God!

Your hands can do so many amazing things if you learn and practice. You can play music, you can write stories, you can paint pictures, you can build things, you can help a friend, or you can even bake cookies!

But, your hands can do bad things also if you're not careful. That is why God wants you to use your hands to do what is right and to do what is helpful.

God put a lot of potential inside of you. This means, you have special power and special abilities waiting to grow out of you! But, to grow into all that God made you to be, you have to be willing to learn things, practice doing things, and working hard.

God wants His children to do their best things—at school, at home, and when you are helping other people.

God gave you the power to do amazing things. And, so when you do your best things, other people notice, and it shows them how great God is, Who made you! You are full of God's purpose, and so the world needs to see what God put inside of you!

Questions:

1. How did God make you?
2. What can your hands can do?
3. Why should we use our hands to do good things?
4. What does it mean to have "potential?"
5. Why is it good to do your best in everything you do?

Memory Verse

"I will praise You, for I am fearfully and wonderfully made; Marvelous are Your works..." Psalm 139:14(NKJV)

Activity: Handy Work!

Supplies: Paper, crayons or colored markers, and your own two hands!

Instructions:

1. Draw around your hands on a piece of paper.
2. In each paper hand, draw or write some things you can do with your hands that help other people (like drawing, helping, hugging, cleaning, ...).
3. Color your paper hands with bright and happy colors!
4. Put your drawing where it can remind you to use your hands to do good things every day.

Notes:

LESSON 48: I NEED THE KINGDOM OF GOD

Learning Objectives:

By the end of this lesson, children will be able to:

1. Understand that the Kingdom of God is a place of peace, a place of joy, a place of love, a place where God is the King.

2. Recognize that their life in God's Kingdom, brings them true happiness and true peace.

3. Explain that we are made to live in God's Kingdom, and that we help to build His Kingdom with all we have.

4. Identify ways they can help to bring God's Kingdom to Earth, like being kind to people, being honest, being loving, and by using their special gifts to help other people.

5. Understand that the whole world needs God's Kingdom. That it is the only way to fix problems; and to bring God's peace to

Comprehension Text:

Did you know, that man cannot live without the Kingdom? We are God's Kingdom builders by nature; and that is the only thing we know how to do. Every day we are building a kingdom—either we build our own little Kingdom; or we build the devil's kingdom, or we build God's Kingdom.

The truth is, we must only build God's Kingdom. This is a place, where God is the King, and where He is in charge of everything.

God made us to live in His Kingdom. He made us to help Him build His Kingdom here on Earth too. So, we are to bring His love, bring His truth, and bring His goodness into our families, into our schools, and into our neighborhoods. When people forget about God's Kingdom, things don't go well for them. Those families will have lots of problems.

They will have no love. Brothers will hate each other, their countries will fight, and their schools' will fail. Poverty and hunger will be there. Sickness and natural disasters will also be there! All their things get out of control!

In the Bible, King David said (NKJV): **"One thing I have desired of the LORD, that I will seek: That I may dwell in the house of the LORD all the days of my life..."** *Psalm 27:4a.*

So, we need God's Kingdom. God's Kingdom is the answer to all the problems in the whole world.

Questions:

1. What is the Kingdom of God?
2. What can we do to help God build His Kingdom here, on Earth?
3. What happens when people forget about God's Kingdom?
4. Why do we need the Kingdom of God?

SECTION 1: PART 3 - WHERE DID I COME FROM?

LESSON 48: I NEED THE KINGDOM OF GOD

Memory Verse

"But seek first the kingdom of God and His righteousness, and all these things shall be added to you."
Matthew 6:33 (NKJV)

 Activity: God's Kingdom

Supplies: Blocks, Legos, or other building toys

How to do this:

1. Use your blocks or Legos to build a special place called, "God's Kingdom."
2. While you build it, think how you can bring God's love and God's kindness to your family, to your school, and to your friends.
3. When you finish building, tell how you can help build God's Kingdom, by being loving and being kind every day.

Notes:

LESSON 49: GOD SENT ME TO DO HIS WORK

Learning Objectives:

By the end of this lesson, children will be able to:

1. Understand that God has a special plan for their life.
2. Explain that their most important job is to do the work God gave them to do for Him.
3. Recognize that even kids can do great things for God, by using their special talents and by showing kindness to other people.
4. Describe ways they can show God's love to other people, like telling people about Jesus or by being a good friend.
5. Feel encouraged and confident that God helps them do their special work for Him They can start right now, to do their special work for God.

Comprehension Text:

When God decided to send you here, to Earth, it was to solve a specific problem. This is something that only you can do to help fix.

Some people spend all their time just trying to make some money or to get by. They forget that the most important thing—the special work which God gave them to do for Him. They work and work, but still they don't feel happy inside. That is, because they are not doing what God sent them to do here.

But here is the good news: God promises to take care of us, so we don't have to worry all the time. That way, we can focus on our special calling—the work God wants us to do for Him.

Even if you're a child, you have a calling to do!

Ephesians 2:10a says **"For we are His workmanship, created in Christ Jesus for good works..."**

This means, you can love other people. You can tell people all about Jesus. You can help your family. You can be a good friend. You can use your talents for God.

God put His Kingdom inside you. So, when you do the good things God made you to do, other people can see God's love and His power shining through you! You're never too little to do big things for God. You can start doing big things for God, right now!

Questions:

1. Did God have a plan for you before you were born?
2. Why do some people feel unhappy, even if they a lot of work to do?
3. What does God promise to do for us?
4. What are some special things you can do for God?
5. Are you too little to do big things for God?

Memory Verse

"I can do all things through Christ who strengthens me."
Philippians 4:13(NKJV)

Activity: My Very Special Work

Supplies: Paper, crayons or colored markers, stickers (optional)

How to do this:

1. Draw a big heart in the middle of your paper.
2. Inside the heart, write or draw some good things you can do to help other people to show God's love (like helping family, being kind, telling other people about Jesus).
3. Decorate your poster with bright colors and stickers.
4. Hang your poster where you can see it every day, so it can remind you that God sent you to do His special work!

Notes:

LESSON 50: NOBODY ELSE CAN DO WHAT I DO

Learning Objectives:

By the end of this lesson, children will be able to:

1. Understand that they are unique and special, made by God to be one of a kind.
2. Explain that God gave them a special job that only they can do, even if other people have the some talents.
3. Recognize that they are part of God's royal family, and so they have a big role to play in His big plan for them to do for Him.
4. Identify ways they can take care of the Earth by using their special gifts and one of a kind talents.
5. Feel confident that what they do, really matters to God, and that using their special gifts, they can shine God's light in the big world out there.

Comprehension Text:

You are one of a kind! No one else in the whole world is the same as you! God gave you a special job that only you can do. Maybe someone else has some of the same talents, but no one can use their talents like you do.

The Bible says, you are part of God's royal family. You are chosen to do a big job for Him. God made people to take care of the Earth.

This means, He gave you the ability to choose well, to fix problems, to make new things, and to be a leader in your own place.

What you do, and how you do it, is very important to God's big plan. When you use your special gifts for God, you shine His light into the whole world!

Questions:

1. Are you like anyone else in the whole world?
2. What kind of family does the Bible say you are part of?
3. What job did God give people to do here, on Earth?
4. Can kids be important to God's plan? Why?
5. How do you shine God's light when you use your special gifts?

Memory Verse

"But you are a chosen generation, a royal priesthood..." 1 Peter 2:9a (NKJV)

Activity: My Special Gift

Supplies: Paper, crayons or colored markers

How to do this:

1. Draw a big gift box on your paper.

2. Inside the box, draw or write some special things God made you to do or be good at doing for Him.
3. Color your gift box bright and beautiful!
4. Share your special gift box with your family or show it to your friend, and tell them how God made you special for Him.

Notes:

LESSON 51: GOD NEEDS ME HERE ON EARTH

Learning Objectives:

By the end of this lesson, children will be able to:

1. Understand that after God made the Earth with all the wonderful things, like animals, plants, and rocks, He gave people the special job to look after the Earth and it's all creatures.

2. Recognize that they need to use their hands, use their brains, and use their creativity to help look after the world around them.

3. Describe ways they can work hard, and how they can help God to build His Kingdom here on Earth.

4. Know that God wants to use them to make the Earth a better, just like it is in Heaven.

Comprehension Text:

God made the Earth full of amazing things—He made the fish, the birds, the animals, the trees, the rocks, and the metals!

But guess what? None of these things can do anything for us, unless we work with them.

If trees could build a house all by themselves—wouldn't that be cool? But we have to use our hands, use our brains, and use our creativity to make things happen. That is because God gave us a special job: to look after the whole Earth, and use its things wisely.

In the Bible, God told us to rule over the fish, rule over the birds, rule over the animals, and rule over everything on the whole earth. This means, we must look after God's creation, and we must use all things to build God's Kingdom.

We can only do this, if we work with God, and if we think creatively, and if we develop and use all the special gifts He gave to us.

God wants to work through you to make His Kingdom big on Earth!

Questions:

1. What kind of amazing things did God make on Earth?
2. Can trees or animals build houses by themselves?
3. What special job did God give us to do?
4. Why do we need to work with God, and be creative like Him?
5. How can you help look after the Earth?

Memory Verse

"And God blessed them, and God said to them, 'Be fruitful and multiply; fill the earth and subdue it...'" Genesis 1:28a (NKJV)

Activity: Earth Care Collage

Supplies: Paper, magazines or printed pictures, scissors, glue, crayons or colored markers

How to do this:

1. Cut out pictures of animals, trees, people helping the Earth (like planting trees, picking up trash), or anything that shows caring for the Earth.
2. Glue the pictures on your paper to make a collage called "Earth Care."
3. Draw or write one way you can help look after the Earth.
4. Show your collage to your family, and tell them why it's important to care for God's creation.

Notes:

LESSON 52: THE EARTH IS MY PERMANENT HOME

Learning Objectives:

By the end of this lesson, children will be able to:

1. Understand that God made the Earth a beautiful, special home for us to live in forever.
2. Tell how sin separated us from God, but that Jesus helps us come back to Him.
3. See that following Jesus, means living with love, living with kindness, living with forgiveness, and living with truth.
4. Tell how that even though the world isn't perfect now, God promises we will live with Him on Earth forever.
5. Say Bible verses which teach about living and reigning with

Comprehension Text:

When God made the Earth, He made it a beautiful and special home for us. He filled it with trees, rivers, mountains, animals, and everything we need to live, grow, and have fun.

The Earth was not just a place to visit—it was to be our forever home where we could walk with God, and look after everything He had made.

But a long time ago, a sad thing happened. Adam, the first man, did not listen to God. That choice brought sin into the world. Sin, means doing things God says not to do.

Sin makes a big wall between us and God. This is why we feel something is missing inside us. We can have fun toys, games, and friends, but our hearts might still feel empty. That is because our spirits were made to live with God, not be away from Him.

The good news is God never gives up on us! He sent His only Son, Jesus, to show us how to come back home, to the Kingdom of God where we belong. When we accept Jesus, we live the Kingdom way—showing God's love, His kindness, His forgiveness, and His truth. Then we start to feel at home again, even when the world isn't perfect.

Some people think our forever home is only far away, in heaven. But the Bible says something amazing in Revelation 5:10(NKJV), it says **"And have made us kings and priests to our God; And we shall reign on the earth."** So, guess what? The Earth is not just where we live now—it's where we will live forever with Jesus, our King!

Questions:

1. What did God make the Earth for?
2. What happened when Adam did not listen to God?
3. Why do we sometimes feel like something is missing inside us?
4. Who did God send to help us come back home?
5. Where will we live forever with Jesus?

Memory Verse

"Blessed are the meek, For they shall inherit the earth." Matthew 5:5(NKJV)

Activity: Walking with Jesus

Supplies: Paper, crayons or colored markers

How to do this:

1. Draw a picture of what you think your forever home with Jesus will look like.
2. Also draw things you love about Earth—like trees, animals, rivers, and mountains.
3. Then draw yourself happy and walking with Jesus.
4. Share your drawing with your family, and tell them why the Earth is our special home.

Notes:

More Books & Resources

DISCIPLING NATIONS SERIES

Kingdom Mandate (for any donation)
Discovering the Lost Kingdom (Volume 1) $14.00
Purpose, Calling, and Gifts (Volume 2) $15.00
God's Original Design (Volume 3) $20.00
Seeing, Entering, and Manifesting the Kingdom of God (Volume 4) $20.00
The Ekklesia (Volume 5) $30.00
The Gospel of the Kingdom (Volume 6) $20.00
Power and Authority of the Church (Volume 7) $15.00
Kingdom Family (Volume 8) $15.00
The Birthing of a Kingdom Nation (Volume 9) $20.00
What Happened to God? (Volume 10) $20.00
7 Dimensions and Operations of the Kingdom of God (Volume 11) $15.00
Kingdom Economy (Volume 12) $15.00
Kingdom Government (Volume 13) $15.00
Releasing Kings and Queens into God's Original Intent (Volume 14) $10.00
Kingdom Secrets to Restoring Nations Back to God (Volume 15) $20.00
Keys to Fulfilling Your Kingdom Assignment (Volume 16) $20.00

KINGDOM LIVING SERIES

The Three Most Important Decisions of Your Life $15.00
Recognizing God's Timing for Your Life $12.00
Overcoming the Spirit of Poverty $10.00
Seven Kinds of Believers $10.00
7 Dimensions of God's Glory $5.00
7 Dimensions of God's Grace $10.00
7 Kinds of Faith $8.00

HEALING OF THE NATIONS SERIES

Principles of Self Governance $20.00

KINGDOM BOOKS FOR KIDS

Genesis 126 Three Volume Book set for boys $25.00
Genesis 126 Three Volume Book set for boys $25.00
Genesis 126 Coloring Books for Boys $15.00
Genesis 126 Coloring Books for Girls $15.00

GENESIS 126 TEACHER'S MANUAL

Level 1 6-8 years $15.00

G126 MOVEMENT
BIBLE STUDY PROGRAM
FOR SUNDAY SCHOOL CHILDREN
AGES: 9-10 YEARS

Level 2 8-10 years $15.00
Level 3 10-12 years $15.00

TO PLACE AN ORDER:

www.TheKingdomNetwork.org
Phone: 1-800-558-5020
Email: info@TheKingdomNetwork.org

Are you struggling to discover your **PURPOSE** ?

You are not supposed to fit in but stand out !

Sign up today for the FREE Online Kingdom Course

DISCOVERING

THE LOST KINGDOM

In this course you'll DISCOVER:

>> Your true identity and purpose
>> What God is doing on the earth and how you can partner with Him in it
>> Why God created the earth and put us on this planet
>> And much more ...

> Why are people becoming more and more disinterested in **church and religion** globally?
> Join the course, and discover
> **what your soul has been searching for all along.**

FREE BOOK AND STUDY GUIDE

Other courses available

>> DISCOVERING PURPOSE, CALLING AND GIFTS
>> SEEING, ENTERING AND MANIFESTING THE KINGDOM
>> GOD'S ORIGINAL DESIGN
>> The Ekklesia
>> The Next move of GOD

And more ...

Register Now @ **www.TheKingdomUniversity.org**

Welcome to
KINGDOM DELIVERANCE
— WORKSHOP —

Are you tired of waiting and looking for breakthroughs? Kingdom of God has the answer.

This kingdom deconstruct workshop is divided into EIGHT major categories which deal with the seven major areas of our life. Each one is connected to the next, and so if one of these areas dysfunctions, it will affect all other areas of your life.

1. Relationship with the Father
2. Spiritual Healing
3. Emotional Healing
4. Purpose and Calling
5. Mastering Gifts and Skills
6. Finances—Learning to Live in Kingdom Economy
7. Healing Relationships
8. Physical Health

Take action now. Order all 8 workshop manuals today!

Thank you so much for taking the courses from The Kingdom University. Taking a course is only the first step. We are pleased to present you with the next step—that of going through the process to get rid of all the extra weights that have been slowing and hindering you from fully living out your kingdom assignment.

Call 1 800 558 5020   www.TheKingdomNetwork.org

www.ingramcontent.com/pod-product-compliance
Lightning Source LLC
Chambersburg PA
CBHW040000080526
44586CB00027B/2831